ORGANIZATIO

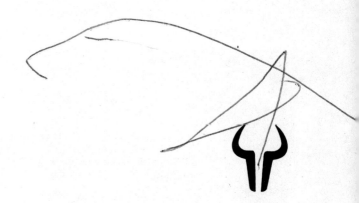

Hutchinson Management Studies Books
Series editor: Peter Lawrence, Senior Lecturer, Loughborough
University of Technology

ORGANIZATIONAL BEHAVIOUR: Politics at Work

Robert Lee and Peter Lawrence

HUTCHINSON

London Melbourne Sydney Auckland Johannesburg

Hutchinson and Co. (Publishers) Ltd
An imprint of the Hutchinson Publishing Group
17-21 Conway Street, London W1P 6JD

Hutchinson Publishing Group (Australia) Pty Ltd
16-22 Church Street, Hawthorn, Melbourne, Victoria 3122

Hutchinson Group (NZ) Ltd
32-34 View Road, PO Box 40-086, Glenfield, Auckland 10

Hutchinson Group (SA) Pty Ltd
PO Box 337, Bergvlei 2012, South Africa

Brookfield Publishing Co., Inc.
Old Post Road, Brookfield, Vermont 05036 USA

First published 1985
© Robert Lee and Peter Lawrence 1985

Set in Plantin 10 on 12pt by AKM Associates (UK) Ltd
Ajmal House, Hayes Road, Southall, London

Printed and bound in Great Britain by
Anchor Brendon Ltd, Tiptree, Essex

British Library Cataloguing in Publication Data
Lee, R.A.
    Organizational behaviour: politics at work. -
    Hutchinson management studies series
    1   Organizational behaviour
    I   Title   II Lawrence, P.A.
    158.7   HD58.7

Library of Congress Cataloguing in Publication Data
Lee, R. A., (Robert Arthur)
Organizational Behaviour
    Includes index.
    1   Organizational Behaviour
    I   Lawrence, Peter A.   II Title
    HD58.7.L44   1985   658.4   85-7835

ISBN   0 09 161651 4

To Maggie
and
To Pat

CONTENTS

theories – Motivation and the political approach – Implications for the practising manager – Conclusion

PREFACE

'Organizational Behaviour' or 'OB' is not yet a neatly defined academic discipline. In the current literature it has a wide range of definitions and there is a confusing array of related subjects and alternative or overlapping names, including human resource management, organization theory, industrial psychology, industrial sociology, personnel management and human relations.

In its broadest sense OB is the study of people in organizations. We do not propose to describe all the different emphases which the inquisitive student will find. It is easier if we just say what we propose to do.

It will soon become clear to the reader that our treatment is not entirely the conventional textbook restatement, albeit in simplified form, of available material from specialist writers. We *will* be describing much fundamental OB theory, however, and will assume no prior knowledge. Where this book differs from many others is in the underlying framework used to analyse and build on OB concepts. By making assumptions about people and organizations which are different from those usually made we mean to throw new light on old topics, bringing them much closer to the fascinating reality of modern organizations. We believe the new approach to OB which is beginning to emerge in the literature, and which forms the basis of this book, will equip the future manager much better for the trials which lie ahead than the simplistic approach of most existing texts.

So what is new about this book on OB? The newness stems from two things. First, the general perspective which we adopt has not been used before to develop a comprehensive textbook. This perspective is known as the political approach; it will be introduced in Chapter 2. Broadly, the organization is conceived of as a coalition of different interest groups which are competing and co-operating as they pursue a variety of ends. No prior right is given to any of the parties involved in the organization to have their own way. As Chapter 1 will show, previous perspectives have tended to be 'managerialist', concerned with some, often unspecified, measures of 'effectiveness' and 'efficiency' towards which the manager *should* be working for the good of the organization. We are concerned with what happens in practice.

The second aspect of newness concerns the ideas about people which are built into our approach. People are characterized primarily as active and goal-seeking, rather than passive and need-orientated. It is one of our hopes for this book that the reader, having emerged at the other end, will never again be a passive pawn to be manoeuvred unknowingly in the organizational political milieu.

Robert Lee
Peter Lawrence

STRUCTURE

The first part of *Organizational Behaviour: Politics at Work* reviews the development of ideas about organizations. The classical writings of Fayol and Taylor provide the foundations for understanding many management concepts, and the human relations perspective of Mayo pushes people into the foreground where they belong. By considering organizations as systems, a new set of variables and relationships can be explored, adding to the picture and developing deeper insights. Contingency theorists have picked out some of these variables, including structure, environment and technology, and shown how their study can further improve our ability to understand and manage. Finally, in Part One, the political approach is presented as the next logical development in organization theory, the next step on the road to reality.

In Part Two we will take three chapters to discuss some of the major aspects of modern OB – motivation, group dynamics and organization structures, cultures and climates. The reader will find a broad overview of these subjects in terms of conventional theories and concepts, yet this will be developed using the political approach to create new interpretations and insights. Each of these chapters finishes with a discussion of its implications for the practising manager.

Part Three is about influencing behaviour, and it is at this point that the political approach is expanded and developed. The four chapters in this section will discuss the different bases of power and how they operate, the context of the political process and its different facets, political strategy formulation, and how to understand and develop strategy in specific political situations. We hope that by the end of his journey the reader will be well equipped to contemplate his place in any political milieu and have a chance to actively influence the behaviour of others.

The book closes with a short Epilogue. Having set aside the subject of ethics in order to develop, without inhibition, the valuable insights which may be gained from the political model, a major point is made – theories can be amoral but managers cannot.

'BOXES'

The political perspective is introduced for the first time in the last part of Chapter 2. During the next three chapters it underlies much of the commentary and critique of contemporary OB. Also, specific aspects of the approach are gradually developed where they build on, or relate to, conventional ideas. The core of the perspective, however, is not given full treatment until Part Three.

To stimulate the reader's interest in what is to come, 'boxes' have been inserted at strategic points in the text during Parts One and Two. These are all headed 'A Rethink . . .' and deal with some issue related to OB. They serve three additional functions: to emphasize points being made in the text, to introduce ideas which will be dealt with in more detail later and to make points which are relevant but not made elsewhere.

The reader is invited to browse through the boxes before starting to tackle the text. He or she will get the flavour of what lies within.

*POLITICAL MAN

- Political man knows what he wants. He knows his own strengths and limitations; he decides on his goals.

- Political man understands the environment in which he finds himself. In fact he chooses his situation for the benefits it provides. He knows the systems, the rules, the pressures, the opportunities and the threats. He is fully conversant with all the circumstances.

- Political man studies his rivals; he can see the situation from their point of view. He identifies their goals and the strategies they may pursue.

- Political man has contacts. He has friends and allies with whom he co-operates for mutual benefit.

- Political man thinks through his strategies, he assesses a range of options in terms of costs, risks and outcomes. He considers any undesirable side-effects or aftermath.

- Political man takes action.

- Political man gets his way – more often than most.

* No sexism intended. The masculine form is used purely in line with publishing convention.

PART ONE

UNDERSTANDING ORGANIZATIONS:

In this first part of *Organizational Behaviour: Politics at Work* we will take two chapters to review the development of ideas about organizations. This is a necessary stepping stone on the way to understanding people in organizations. We will see that there are several different 'organization theories' which provide a range of different frameworks for thinking, and help us to identify some of the key concepts to be given more detailed treatment later. We will see how organization structure, individual motivation, group behaviour, interpersonal influence, and other important facets of organization life have formed parts of the major theories of other writers, and we will discuss the strengths and limitations of each perspective.

In the latter part of Chapter 2 the reader is introduced to the political perspective which underlies the body of the book. By then he will have learned about earlier perspectives and will be able to fully appreciate how the new approach differs.

1

CLASSICAL, HUMAN RELATIONS AND SYSTEMS APPROACHES

In this chapter we briefly describe the development of organization theory. The 'Classical' ideas of early management writers are discussed and the 'Human Relations' approach is introduced as the foundation for modern OB. The widely used 'Systems' theme is explored and presented as underpinning the conventional wisdom about organizations. The term 'managerialism' is explained and its consequences examined.

Organization theory

Organization theory is the study of ways of thinking about organizations. Within this subject area there are many different schools of thought, with a range of contrasting and conflicting ideas, and we shall be examining three of the major ones in this chapter.

Some of the important questions which any theory of organizations must tackle are:

- What are the key variables which determine what happens in organizations?
- What goals does, or should, an organization pursue?
- How is the organization co-ordinated or bound together?
- What assumptions can we make about the motivation and behaviour of the people in the organization?

Everyone who has experience of formal organizations has some kind of organization theory. It may be implicit, only part formed, inconsistent, but it is none the less there, influencing the individual's perception of what goes on around him and his behaviour. When the individual is a manager it is important for him to be aware of his personal theory in order that he can act reasonably in a range of situations, and also develop his ideas as new experiences provide feedback on how useful his view of the organizational world is. Without this kind of personal organization theory the manager would just respond unpredictably to new circumstances and would be unable to make sense of the complex environment in which he works.

A rethink: The manager

A Manager is someone called a Manager. The term is, in fact, hard to define. Often, it means that he supervises other employees or is in charge of important systems or tasks, but this may also be true of employees who are not called Managers.

Sometimes a Manager is thought to have particular responsibilities for 'efficiency', 'productivity' or 'profit'. He is seen as part of the company rather than a mere employee who works for it.

In political terms a Manager is simply someone with the title. But we should note that it tends to carry with it certain powers and privileges. Managers usually earn higher salaries than non-managers and often have better conditions of employment. Managerial job descriptions often specify rights to spend money, recruit people, give orders and other such useful, political possibilities.

Managers are often ambitious. This means they wish to rise up the formal hierarchy, acquiring more power and privileges on the way. In order to reach the higher levels they may have to conform to the behaviours desired by those who are there already. This may mean wearing the right clothes and expressing the right beliefs, as well as achieving the right levels of performance. On reaching the higher levels the Manager may be able to change organizational systems to influence the behaviour of those around and below him. Until that time he will usually wish to at least *seem* to be conforming to expectations, otherwise he is unlikely to progress.

Different writers on organizations also have their individual theories. To simplify study of their ideas we assemble them into 'schools of thought' – groups of people with similar answers to the questions asked earlier. They tend to have attitudes in common and make comparable assumptions. This is an over-simplification because often writers within each school are at odds on some points but it is still a useful way to structure our thinking.[1]

The classical approach to understanding organizations

During the nineteenth century the environment of economic organizations changed drastically. Technologies became more sophisticated and their rate of development began to increase; markets became more competitive as other countries industrialized and as customers became more discerning; trade unions emerged as a force in both politics and industry and the government itself began to influence the activities of organizations more and more with laws and economic measures.

The Limited Liability Acts passed in the mid nineteenth century in Britain meant that investors did not have to become partners and risk their total wealth. They could buy shares and only involve themselves in the business to the extent of making that limited financial commitment. It was this development, coupled with the need to cope with the increasingly complex environment and the increasing size of organizations, which led to the emergence of a new 'managerial class'. These people, while not owning a significant part of the organization, had the power to control it. It is this managerial class which nowadays, by its cumulative actions, exerts perhaps the greatest influence over the nature of our society.

The first view of organizations which we must examine is that put forward by their earliest spokesmen. In part it reflects the needs of the day and the different environment of organizations in an earlier period; this makes the model appear oversimple but it is where our forerunners started, and it is where we must start, not just for historical reasons but because the past has had a formative effect on the present.

The early 'spokesmen' for the new managers were usually experienced and successful managers themselves. They were aware of the problems of their colleagues in coping with the new circumstances we have outlined, and they attempted to synthesize their experience systematically into an easily learned model of the organization and a simple set of rules for improving its performance. This is known as the classical approach and it is represented in Figure 1.

The classical view portrays the organization as an instrument for making profit

Figure 1 *The classical model*

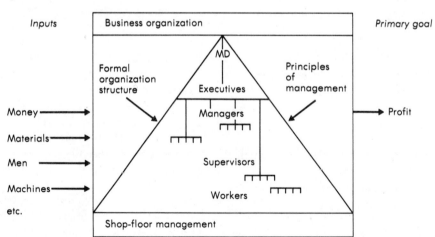

for the owners. The purpose of management is to convert inputs – men, money, materials, and so on – into profit via good managerial practice.

Some writers focus on the 'shop-floor' end of the organization, concentrating on the jobs people do, the payment systems, work layout, supervision and related areas. The most influential ideas on these subjects originated with an American, Frederick Winslow Taylor, whose work we shall briefly examine.[2]

The other group of classical writers deals with the higher management levels of the organization. These writers are mostly concerned with formal structure (or hierarchy) and the processes of general management. They attempt to specify a number of principles which should be followed if efficiency is to be achieved. Most later writers in this genre have built on the work of a Frenchman, Henri Fayol.[3]

Shop-floor management – F.W. Taylor

F.W. Taylor served an engineering apprenticeship from 1874 to 1878. He took a Mechanical Engineering degree and then became a chief engineer for the Midvale Steel Company, eventually moving to become general manager of a paper mill. In 1893 he opened an office in New York as a consulting engineer and it was after this that his ideas on what he called 'scientific management' were published. He is probably the best known and most influential of all management theorists.

Taylor's first major concept is the separation of planning from doing. Employees were seen as unsuited to the making of decisions in terms of both ability and motivation. Planning and decision-making should be passed up the hierarchy to the better qualified managers who will have the best interests of the company at heart.

This leads directly to the second major idea, job design. Taylor believed in the maximum fragmentation of work. Tasks should be divided into their simplest possible constituent elements and each worker should do as few elements as can be conveniently combined into a job. This de-skilling process was seen to have advantages such as minimizing training time, making recruitment easier, making it easier to organize work into flow lines, and removing undesirable decision-making from shop-floor workers. There would be less problems to cause errors, and workers could become incredibly quick at their simple tasks.

There can be no doubt that the widespread application of this philosophy has led to great improvements in productivity. There are problems associated with it, however. Workers doing simple, undemanding tasks may become unsatisfied, bored, frustrated with their jobs and antipathetic to the company. This can lead to a range of human and industrial relations problems. In the 1980s we are witnessing a technological revolution in which microprocessor-based machines are taking over many Taylorian routine tasks. The long-run effects of this process are still the subject of speculation.

Simplifying jobs paves the way for what is perhaps Taylor's greatest contribution to management – Time Study. Time study involves a number of different techniques for calculating how long a qualified worker of average ability and motivation should take to do a job. Nowadays it has been developed into a very fine art and is combined with Method Study aimed at finding the best method for doing the job. Times from time studies are useful for calculating such things as costs, delivery dates, and machine loading, as well as for balancing the work done by each operator on a flow line. For Taylor, however, the main purpose of these times was to form the basis of payments by results systems.

If we know how long the average worker should take, then we can pay people more if they work faster and less if they work slower. In terms of motivation the assumption is that people will work as fast as they can to earn as much as they can. This may, to some extent, be a self-fulfilling effect of Taylor's approach to management. Since the only thing people can get from their de-skilled jobs is money, it is most likely to be their prime work motivation. Taylor's model relies on a view of the worker as a cog in the organizational machine, fitting neatly into a carefully designed job and working hard for the prospect of greater income. Other aspects of human motivation and behaviour are assumed unimportant or controllable. As we shall see, this is much too simple a view.

Formal organization and general processes of management

Henri Fayol was the first of an influential group of writers who were concerned about the ways in which higher-level managers should be organized into the hierarchy and should carry out their tasks. Fayol was appointed as Chief Engineer at a colliery in 1860 and six years later he became manager. In a further six years he became general manager and ultimately he was made managing director of the whole mining combine. During his time as managing director he turned the company round from near bankruptcy to financial success. After his retirement in 1918 he decided to synthesize his experience into a form which would be useful to other managers.

Fayol identified five elements of managerial work which constitute probably the first notable definition of management. For him it consisted of planning, organization, command, co-ordination and control. These are all still considered vital elements of modern management although many writers would make changes, adding aspects such as communicating, motivating, decision-making and others.

Following Fayol's pattern, most classical writers summarize their ideas about the processes and structure of management into lists of principles. Fayol saw them just as useful guidelines, but later writers have presented them as universal prescriptions for success.[4]

The most fundamental of all classical concepts is authority. This can be simply described as the right to get things done. The classical writers were keen to legitimate their position of influence, and it is partly in this light that one of their major propositions, that authority originates entirely with ownership, must be viewed. They see authority as being given by the owners to the board of directors, who in turn delegate it to the managing director, and so on down to the shop floor.

A full understanding of authority is vital to the philosophy of the new approach on which this book is based, and it will be returned to later. At this stage we may just note the inadequacy of the classical idea that having formal authority is sufficient to enable a manager to get people to work effectively. If subordinates choose not to co-operate with a manager, or not to maximize effort, then the sources of influence he has over them may be varied and complex. Equally they may have sources of influence over him, such as restricting information, approaching other managers, or taking collective action. As we shall see, *power* is a more practical variable for the manager to use, authority is just one of its facets.

Related to authority is the idea of responsibility. This is seen as the obligation to undertake tasks. In classical principle one should not have authority without commensurate responsibility and *vice versa*. Having created these building blocks the classical writers develop the idea of hierarchy. Gulick for instance sees organizing as 'interrelating the subdivisions of work by allotting them to men who are placed in a structure of authority, so that the work may be co-ordinated by orders of superiors to subordinates, reaching from the top to the bottom of the entire enterprise'.[5]

The importance of co-ordination is emphasized by Mooney and Reiley: 'There

---

A rethink: Authority

Authority in business organizations is seen by many management writers as originating with ownership. Clearly we do recognize in our society the rights of owners to use their property more or less as they wish. We also, however, recognize other fundamental rights: the rights of labour for example, and basic human rights, and these may also operate in organizations.

The rights-of-ownership argument may be diminished when we realize that most shares are held by institutions such as unit trusts and pension funds who have little interest in the day-to-day affairs of management. Furthermore, the purchase of shares in a company actually gives the shareholder, even if he were motivated, very little influence over the activities of the existing management.

In political terms, authority involves rights given by people to other people – on whatever basis they choose. Often subordinates have been so conditioned that they simply do not question the authority of their supervisor any more than they question that of their parents or their teachers.

In this view, authority cannot exist between a superior and subordinate unless it is recognized by the subordinate.

must be orderly arrangement of group effort, to provide unity of action in the pursuit of a common purpose.'

Below we note the general statements of some of the remaining more central classical principles:

Organizational balance: The relative size and importance of each department should remain consistent with its desired contribution to organizational objectives.

Unity of command: No member of an organization should receive orders from more than one superior.

Exception principle: Decisions which recur frequently should be reduced to a routine and delegated to subordinates, and only those which are non-recurring should be referred to superiors.

Span of control: This principle concerns the number of subordinates who should report to one superior – usually felt to be five or six.[7]

Other principles from more recent classical writers concern the grouping of activities together into functions, the ideas of centralization and decentralization, and a range of management processes from communication to decision-making.

On first reading, the common-sense logic of classical principles is appealing. It would be foolish to deny their usefulness. They are often helpful first approximations to what goes on in organizations and they have the merit, particularly important for early generations of managers, of being easy to understand. Their weakness is in application. They are universal prescriptions about what *should* happen rather than descriptions about reality. This renders them both too simple and too general for easy transfer into actual organizations with their wide range of technologies, markets, sizes and other differences. Urwick, one of Fayol's most quoted disciples, is unaware of this problem: 'These principles can be studied as a technical question, irrespective of the purpose of the enterprise, the personnel composing it, or any constitutional, political or social theory underlying its creation.[8]

The classical writers do not deal with the issue of change and how to cope with it. Theirs is a static approach, designing a detailed rigid organization. In a situation of constant threat, competition, technical development or growth it may not be desirable to take decision-making away from lower-level employees, or to impose tightly defined limitations on tasks and authority – this possibility is ignored.

The classical philosophy of both Fayol and Taylor is one of consensus. Employees come to work primarily to maximize wages, and management need to design the jobs, the organization and the payment systems so that if people work hard they will do just that. If management has done its job properly, then the increased efforts of the workers will mean higher productivity, higher profits and ultimately higher dividends to the owners. Everybody wins – workers get high wages, owners get high dividends, and managers are happy because they have done their job well. This entirely neglects the conflicts of interests and attitudes

A rethink: The formal hierarchy

The formal hierarchy of authority which most people perceive to exist within an organization can be viewed as one of the attempts used by senior managers to influence the behaviour of organization members.

The hierarchy is built up of job descriptions, rights, privileges and obligations. Position in the hierarchy affects access to information, people, materials and systems, all of which may affect ability to influence others.

Most people just accept their job description as being what they *should* do and they accept their superior's right to give them instructions because of his position in the hierarchy. But it is often valuable to remember that job descriptions and hierarchies are created by people for the pursuit of purposes which *they* wish to see achieved. The individual who does the job and who is part of the hierarchy may disagree with the purposes for which they were designed, or he may dislike their effects on him. This may lead him to behave in ways not desired by those who set them up. If he does this he will need to be careful because there is much power within the hierarchy. Failure to conform can lead to sanctions such as being passed over for promotion and wage rises, and eventually to dismissal.

which exist in the business organization, and one result of it is the failure of these theorists to deal with trade unions and the part they play in industrial life.

A further criticism of this approach is its treatment of people. They are portrayed crudely as money-motivated automatons who are happy with repetitive, unskilled work. Further, there are seen to be two classes of people: the managers are more broadly motivated than the rest, they are prepared to take on challenges, to plan and make decisions; these are the people who should co-ordinate and control the activities of the majority, a 'them and us' philosophy.

The classical model is thus about how a group of experienced managers would like to see organizations operate.

The idea of a machine-like business in which people are the cogs, performing according to their job descriptions, using their prescribed authority, working in carefully balanced departments to achieve carefully worked out goals is not bad as a simple model, but it provides only the bare bones of understanding. The classical writers give the impression that there is no need for the manager to understand the true complexities of organizational life, because these have been worked out by the present writer and taken into account when developing his particular principles. For the modern student of management there is no such easy answer;

he is concerned with reality. In the next section we will take another step along the road.

The human relations approach to understanding organizations

The First World War brought about change in the tone of many British management writings. The sacrifices of the working class and the co-operativeness of the trade unions were vital to the war effort. Many restrictive practices were ended; 'dilution' of skilled jobs with unskilled workers and transfers of workers to key industries were permitted; and the right to strike was forgone for the duration of the war. This led to calls for a 'new start' to industrial relationships when hostilities had ceased.[9]

Writers such as Lee, Sheldon, Cadbury and Rowntree began to emphasize the employees' needs for 'fairness', 'justice' and friendly supervision.[10] They criticized Taylor on human grounds, such as the physical strain and psychological undesirability of 'de-skilling' and 'speeding up'. Sheldon, for example, prescribed that management should provide interesting and challenging work whenever possible, reduce unrewarding, exhausting toil to a minimun, and regard the worker as an individual.[11]

These writers, however, had little influence on management practice. The short post-war boom was followed by a severe depression, and the General Strike of 1926 emphasizes the state of industrial relations during that period. Nevertheless they anticipated many of the ideas of the American human relations writers of the 1920s due to their similar discontent with the treatment of people by classical writers.

The Hawthorne Studies

A major focal point for early human relations concepts was the Hawthorne Studies conducted by Elton Mayo and his colleagues at the Hawthorne Plant of the Western Electric Company between April 1927 and August 1932.[12] This famous research programme has since been criticized for its obvious methodological and conceptual eccentricities[13]. We should not underestimate its symbolic significance, however, as a turning point in management theory.

In November 1920, industrial engineers (the disciples of Taylor) at the Hawthorne Plant began a series of experiments to determine the optimum lighting intensity for a group of 120 girls who were assembling relays for use in telephone switchboards.

Two groups of workers had been isolated and the lighting conditions for one were varied and for the other held constant. No significance differences in output were found between the two; indeed, whatever was done with the lighting, production rose in both groups.

Elton Mayo and his team heard about this phenomenon and were invited to investigate further. We shall outline two of the major elements of Mayo's study.

1   The Relay Assembly Test Room (RATR) Experiments   It was decided that, instead of lighting, a new factor in the work context of the girls should be measured – the hours of work (including tea breaks and lunch periods). Six girls were placed in a separate test room after their output had been secretly measured in the large group. They were given a medical check and told to work naturally throughout the experiment. They were also allowed to make suggestions about the test room conditions and arrangements. One of the researchers was located in the room as an observer.

Approximately every two months for two years the girls' conditions of work were changed. Output increased with each change made.

The next stage in the experiment was to return to the original conditions. The operatives reverted to a forty-eight hour, six day week. Output went up to the highest yet recorded. By this time it was 30 per cent above the base level. The explanation eventually given for this behaviour was that the girls experienced a tremendous increase in work satisfaction because they had greater freedom in their working environment and control over their own pace-setting. The six operatives had become a social group with their own standards and expectations. Mayo's generalization was that work satisfaction depends to a large extent on the informal social pattern of the work group. Where norms of co-operativeness and high output are established because of a feeling of importance, physical conditions have little impact.

The observer had noted increased friendliness and group spirit amongst the girls, and he in turn became involved in this process. He came to intervene between the girls and their supervisor in a 'surrogate supervisor' role. This led Mayo to conclude that the two important areas of social work relationships are within the work group and between workers and supervisor.

2   The Bank Wiring Observation Room (BWOR)   The second phase of the Hawthorne experiments involved observation of a group performing a task in a 'natural' setting. Fourteen men were involved in the wiring, soldering and inspection of banks of equipment; an observer was placed in the room. Eventually the men began to ignore the observer's presence and work 'normally'. The researchers made several interesting discoveries about their behaviour which many readers will be able to relate to their own experiences.

The group as a whole had certain codes of conduct or 'norms' of behaviour which were enforced by social pressures. Also the group was socially split into two sub-groups, or cliques, with their own special games, expressions and ways of behaving.

The group at the front of the room considered their work more difficult than that of those at the back and thus felt themselves to be of higher status.

One of the major norms concerned output. Six thousand units was seen as a fair day's work. Despite the fact that the men were on a payment by results scheme they did not attempt to maximize output; instead they aimed for a steady work flow of 6000 units. Some days they would overproduce and not report the surplus until a later date when they underproduced. This was done with the collusion of the inspectors and supervisor.

A second norm was that the formal authority of the inspectors and supervisor should not be emphasized by officious behaviour. One inspector felt himself to be superior and his life was made so difficult by the men playing tricks on him and other social pressures that he asked to be transferred. Friction within the bank wiring room also arose because some individuals would deviate considerably from the 6000 unit norm. If they underproduced they were called 'chisellers', and if they overproduced they were called 'ratebusters'. They might be subjected to abuse and physical aggression in the form of shoulder bashing or 'biffing'.

There was still more damaging conflict between the two cliques. The low-status clique felt insulted at being looked down on so they underproduced in order to annoy the others.

The BWOR, in contrast to the RATR, provides us with an example of a situation in which the human relations situation is not entirely favourable to high output. It demonstrates that it is not sufficient to design jobs, work situations, hierarchies of authority, and payment systems. People will interact in much more unpredictable and complex ways than in the formal system which might be designed in line with the classical concepts. The early human relations writers called deviations from formally prescribed behaviour the 'informal' organization.

This dichotomizing between what should happen – the formal system – and the additional complications due to informal behaviour, emphasizes the perspective of human relations as building on to classical ideas rather than working against them. The human relations writers saw themselves as putting meat on the classical skeleton. As Kelly states: 'The point about human relations and Taylorism . . . is that they operate on different dimensions, and the continued existence of one in no way entails the demise of the other.'[14] This different dimension is *people*.

Figure 1.2 represents the early human relations approach.

For Huneryager and Heckmann, 'Human Relations is a systematic, developing body of knowledge devoted to explaining the behaviour of individuals in the working organization.'[15] This approach is still very much in evidence today, and rightly so. Without people nothing would happen in the organization. Materials, money, machines, buildings – all would be lifeless without people to convert them into activity and output.

The human relations writers tend to see the organization's goals in terms of more than just profit. It is suggested that management also have an obligation to provide social and psychological satisfactions to employees. They, after all, contribute their labour to the organization and are entitled to fair treatment in return for their efforts. Whilst shareholders tend to be primarily interested in the high dividends and share price which usually result from good profits, employees may want more than just financial rewards. This is the major value underlying the

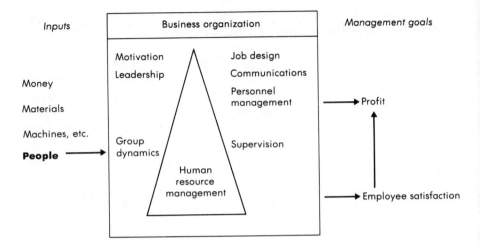

Figure 2   *The human relations model*

human relations philosophy.

It is often argued that providing employee satisfactions such as interesting work, opportunities for promotion and social fulfilment will also lead to increased effort and thus higher profits. Like the classical approach, this too is a consensus model – everybody can have what they want. We should not doubt where ultimate loyalties lie however. Few writers would suggest that the needs of employees should take precedence over profits.

A rethink: Organizational goals

An individual or group may believe they have the right to specify a set of goals for an organization. Others, however, may dispute this right and may believe they should set goals, or perhaps that goal-setting should be a negotiating process. Still others may question the rights of both parties and suggest alternative groups who might be involved. Until there is universal agreement on goals we cannot attribute them to 'the organization'.

Nevertheless, many people believe that organizations do have certain goals and this affects their behaviour. They may, for example, pursue profits and productivity even without the influence mechanisms (such as promotion, job descriptions, etc.) already set up to ensure that they do. It is psychologically convenient to do this because it makes us feel less oppressed by the influence mechanisms of those at the higher levels of the organization.

Human relations is the direct forerunner of modern OB. Its three major subject divisions provide the focuses for Chapters 3, 4 and 5 of this book, in which we shall be reviewing OB as a discipline. We shall be developing new ideas which build on the old foundations before breaking new ground in the later chapters. The three areas are:

1 *The individual* Psychology provides the major academic concepts and theories for considering the individual. Drawing on this discipline, human relations writers have examined such areas as values, beliefs, attitudes, personality, aptitudes and motivation.
2 *The group* Drawing on social psychology, writers have examined such areas as group dynamics, leadership and communication.
3 *The organization* Drawing on sociology to some extent but also developing from the classical writings, human relations writers have examined such areas as organization structure, culture and climate.

The systems approach to understanding organizations

In the 1950s, the roots of modern conventional management thought began to emerge in the literature. The 'Systems Approach', as it is now known, is the dominant framework in most management textbooks; often it is not identified explicitly but is adopted without question. It has achieved the status of a 'dominant paradigm'[16] or a 'conventional wisdom'[17]; in other words, its basic tenets are widely accepted and those who deny or even question them are in danger of being considered heretics. This book is a work of heresy. Let us then briefly outline the way of thinking about organizations which we will later begin to question.

By the Second World War, both classical ideas about management structure and processes, and human relations ideas about supervision and the informal organization, were firmly established. Alongside them were growing bodies of literature about management functions such as production and operations management, finance and accounts, labour management (later to become personnel), sales and distribution (later developed into marketing), and research and development. Neither of the two organization theories made particular contributions to the development of functional specialisms, so they were treated as separate subjects. How strange. It was already recognized that there was more to management than a sound classical hierarchy or satisfied employees and yet it took decades for a theory of organization to emerge which accepted this fact. Such was systems theory. It acknowledged that effective management involves making the right product for the right customers at the right price. It accepted that companies have to survive in a range of environments and cope with complex threats and changes. For the first time we had an approach which explained differences between organizations and why they change over time.

The world in which we live can be viewed as consisting of an enormous number of interlinked 'systems'. These 'systems' may be very small, as are the atoms of which we are composed, or they may be very large, as is the solar system of which our planet forms a part. The systems may be tangible, as is the motor car, or intangible, as are concepts like the legal system. The systems may be natural, like plants and animals, or man-made, like a television.

So what makes all these things systems? Most things can be viewed as systems provided they fulfil some simple criteria. They must be composed of inter-dependent parts or sub-systems. The sub-systems must combine together in some way to form a unit. The unit or system must perform functions for some greater system of which it is a part.

Let us develop a few simple examples. The motor car is composed of a number of parts – the body, the brakes, the steering, the suspension, the engine and so on. These parts are interdependent in that they transmit inputs and outputs to each other and they fit together as a unit. They perform a wide range of different functions which contribute to the total system – the car. We should note that, as is often the case, the system is much more than merely the sum of the parts, it has a character all of its own and can achieve outcomes which could not easily be predicted from a separate knowledge of ignition, transmission, suspension and braking systems. The car is a part of the national transport system, performing a wide range of social and economic functions for society.

The human body, one of the earliest subjects for systems theory, can be viewed as a complex network of interacting sub-systems. The respiratory system, the digestive system, the nervous system, the skeletal system, and so on, all combine together to produce a living, breathing, thinking human being who is, as before, much more than just the sum of his component parts.

The individual whose body has just been viewed in system terms can be viewed as a sub-system of many wider systems. He is a sub-system performing functions for his family, for the economy, for the rugby team perhaps, and so on. He may also, as we shall see, be a sub-system performing useful functions for a business organization.

Some systems, like man-made machine systems, are known as 'closed systems'. This means that the inputs, such as petrol, oil, water and electricity are known, and the system can be arranged to use them in some hopefully predictable way to produce the desired outputs. Other systems, like the economy, are 'open systems'. This means that the inputs, throughputs, and outputs cannot be easily predicted or controlled. Clearly, open systems are much more difficult to deal with. This is an unfortunate fact of life for the business manager.

Figure 3 represents the business organization as a system: on the right hand side is a stepladder representing the organization and its network of interacting sub-systems, and their subsystems, down to the individual employee. The organization performs *functions* for the wider society of which it is a part; it provides taxes, wages, dividends, goods and services, employment and a range of other outputs. For the organization theorist using the systems model, 'functions' usually become 'goals'! At the very least the assumption is made that the organization has an overriding goal of survival. Most exponents of systems theory tend to emphasize

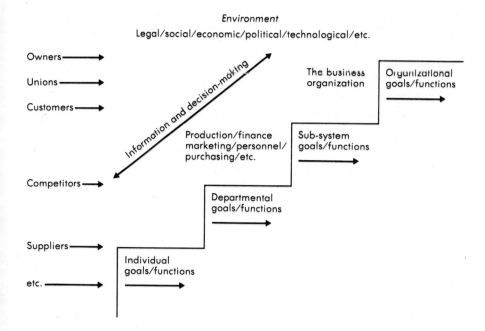

Figure 3   *The systems model*

goals such as profit, sales and market share as pre-eminent. With these in mind they proceed to write about the organization, or whatever aspect they are concerned with, in terms of its contribution to their achievement. Often this orientation is merely implied by the words 'effectiveness' or 'efficiency':

> 'Marketing is the management process which identifies, anticipates and supplies customer requirements efficiently and profitably.'[18]

> 'Personnel administration is . . . organising and treating individuals at work so that they will get the greatest possible realisation of their intrinsic abilities, thus attaining maximum efficiency for themselves and their group, and thereby giving the enterprise of which they are a part its determining competitive advantage and its optimum results.'[19]

> 'Of all the information that is transmitted within a firm and between firms and the community, none is more important than financial information because businesses are run to make a profit. A good accounting system provides this information about money.'[20]

Some writers within the Systems tradition do emphasize the responsibility which the organization has to its owners, its employees, its customers and society at large. However, they rarely state how these responsibilities should be fulfilled, focusing largely on the pursuit of economic efficiency. The problems they would face if they were to tackle the multiple responsibility issue would be twofold. First, many of the objectives of the different parties are hard to identify and measure, and they will vary between organizations. Second, there are underlying incompatibilities between the different objectives which can only be resolved by conflict, competition and compromise. This makes life rather difficult, so most writers prefer to gloss over such considerations and design for the conventional, measurable financial goals. Ansoff summarizes this approach:

> 'For the purpose of discussing business decisions we need only what mathematicians would call a 'weak' assumption, namely, that, however measured and however variable, a set of objectives can be ascribed to each firm, and that this set is the major guidepost in the decision process.'

and

> '. . . essential to an understanding of decision making is that a firm seeks its objectives through the medium of profit.'[24]

Thus, to return to Figure 3, the goals of the business organization are set at the top; these are divided and passed down to the sub-systems such that if each sub-system

---

A rethink: Management textbooks

Most management textbooks assume that the reader wishes to study their branch of management in order to learn how to be a 'better' manager. 'Better' is usually taken for granted to mean 'more productive', 'more profitable', 'more effective' and so on.

These textbooks tend to provide the reader with a picture of what life would be like in organizations if everyone agreed with the writers' views. This can lead to much disillusionment when the student enters the real world. Here he will find conflict, stress, ambition, incompetence, nepotism, unreason and fun – all a fascinating kaleidoscopic turmoil. This is because, despite the best efforts of management courses and texts, people still will not agree with one another over what should be happening in organizations.

No textbook can be unbiased, but if they would all make quite clear what organization theory they are based on, and why, then the reader could evaluate them accordingly; and if they would deal more with what actually happens in organizations as well as what the writer would like to happen, then practising managers would be less disparaging of their content.

Failure to recognize the true political complexity of organizations leads to a failure to search for ways of coping with it.

– marketing, production, etc. – achieves its goals (performs its functions), then the firm will achieve *its* goals. Within each sub-system this process is repeated down to the individual employee.

In order for goals to be realistic and in order for the sub-systems to work together there have to be transfers between them of materials, people and information. One of the great contributions of systems to management has been its special emphasis on information flow and decision-making. O'Shaughnessy describes five steps to designing organizations using the systems approach:

1 Specifying objectives.
2 Determining the sub-systems, or main decision areas.
3 Analysing the decision areas and establishing information needs.
4 Designing the communication channels for the information flow.
5 Grouping decision areas to minimize the communications burden.[22]

Information to assist decision-making does not come only from other sub-systems. Another major contribution of systems is its focus on the environment of the organization. In Figure 3 we have noted some of the key features: the economy in which the company is placed, the technological environment, the laws it has to comply with, and of course the institutions it has to deal with, such as suppliers, competitors and trade unions. The Systems approach tells us that we must have mechanisms for monitoring changes in the environment and communicating them to the relevant sub-systems. It tells us that we must have methods for linking sub-systems so that they will work together not just in a stable environment but also in response to change.

As a manager, then, we would be encouraged by the systems approach to set goals for the organization and commensurate sub-goals for each sub-system. We would concentrate on providing information channels so that good decisions can be made and we would design systems so that sub-systems would work together when necessary. In particular we would ensure that there are mechanisms for bringing about co-operation when changes have to be made. An example will show how organizations can be viewed as adapting systems.

Let us suppose that we are a major manufacturer of a single brand of breakfast cereal aimed at the general family market. In recent years there have been many changes in our environment: the costs of our raw material have risen much faster than those of other breakfast products, competitors have attacked segments of our market with cereals aimed specifically at children, slimmers, and the health food market. New technologies for cereal manufacture have been developed and also new materials and methods for packaging. If we are to survive we will have to respond to these changes.

Different departments are responsible for identifying new threats and opportunities in the various aspects of the environment. They must, however, be integrated sufficiently to work together; perhaps, in this case, in cross-system project teams or new cross-system departments. Research and development engineers, design engineers and marketing managers will work together, perhaps developing a new product. They may design new technology or adapt technology which is available outside the organization. At each stage the new product will be tested in marketing terms. There is no point making it if it will not sell – and at the right price. Accountants will be involved in costing both the product and the production system, and finding the necessary funds. Industrial and production engineers will estimate production times and develop work methods and plans for machine layout and scheduling the work through the production system. Purchasing managers will be confirming the availability of and negotiating contracts for machinery and raw materials. Personnel will be assessing the needs for people in terms of numbers and skills; they will be monitoring the labour market to check that the required manpower is available, and if it is not they will be setting up training systems to produce people who can fill the gaps. Personnel may also be working with the trade unions to set up a job grading system, payment systems and other procedures for the new employees. The unions may need to be involved at every stage of the changes to ensure their acceptance of the new situation. And so it goes on, departments working together, individuals, resources, information, skills and effort all crossing sub-system boundaries in order to ensure that the overall system, the organization, survives and prospers. At the end of the day a new factory, producing a new product, in a modern package, for which the marketing department will create a new image, will emerge from the organization's attempt to adapt to its new circumstances.

Even with this simple example and the brief outline which preceded it we can see the importance of the systems approach. It does not deny the need to design structure or to motivate people, but it balances these with the needs to monitor the environment, integrate organizational sub-systems and make decisions. So what are its deficiencies? What is so wrong with the systems model that we have felt the need to write this book to help correct its influence in the field of OB? The answer lies chiefly in a single word – managerialism.

Managerialism

Earlier in this chapter when introducing the classical writers we portrayed them as representatives of an emerging 'managerial class'. We noted that collectively this group of people, though not *owning* a large proportion of the nation's wealth do have a great deal of *control* over it. Even the individual manager may have authority over valuable assets and considerable amounts of money plus, of course, his subordinates. The early classical writers argued that their authority was delegated to them by the owners, but this has been disputed since the 1930s.[23] John Child summarizes the argument:

'As business enterprises grow they become organisationally and technologically more complex and therefore rely increasingly on the employment of specialist managers. They also issue more share capital as they expand, and this is taken up by a body of shareholders which is rapidly growing both because economic development enables more people to invest in shares and because progressive taxation (and death duties) tends to break up formerly large shareholdings. As share-ownership becomes more dispersed it divides control and this encourages absenteeism from company activities. The consequent power vacuum is filled by an increasingly entrenched management'[24]

The primary 'managerialist' belief is that management controls the business organization with only limited influence from the owners. This limited influence mainly takes the form of a need to pay a certain level of dividend and keep share prices up, but these are constraints rather than objectives to be maximized.

But more importantly managerialism also involves the belief that managers have the right to control the organization and will try to direct it 'efficiently'. Efficiency is rarely explained but we have shown how it is used in the preceding section with the quoted definitions of marketing, personnel and accounting. We have argued that it usually involves the pursuit of financial criteria of performance.

Most managerialists would argue that in the long run this is also the best direction for society.

Thus, for managerialists, organizations have goals which are decided by management and which they have the right to impose.

Managerialism tends to be the underlying ideology for the systems approach to understanding organizations. If there were no goals how could we design systems to achieve them? If there was no direction how could we make decisions, how could we co-ordinate activities, how would we know what information to gather? It is probable that the values embodied in managerialism as we have described it encompass the public position of the vast majority of managers. As far as their actual behaviour is concerned, however, we will argue later that managerialism is a poor model.

References
1   This chapter is a development of ideas first put forward in our earlier book, *Insight Into Management* (Oxford University Press 1984)
2   F.W. Taylor, *Scientific Management* (Harper and Row 1947)
3   H. Fayol, *General and Industrial Management* (Pitman 1949)
4   For example, L. Gulick and L. Urwick, *Papers on the Science of Adminstration* (New York: Institute of Public Administration, Columbia University 1937); and J.D. Mooney and A.C. Reiley, *The Principles of Organization* (New York: Harper 1939).
5   Gulick, in Gulick and Urwick, *Papers on the Science of Administration*, p. 6.
6   Mooney and Reiley, *The Principles of Organization*, p. 4
7   J.L. Massie, 'Management Theory', Chapter 9, p. 398, in J. March, *Handbook of Organisation* (Rand McNally 1966), pp. 387–422
8   Urwick, in Gulick and Urwick, *Papers on the Science of Administration*
9   J. Child, *British Management Thought* (George Allen and Unwin 1969), p. 54

10   *ibid.*, p. 56
11   O. Sheldon, *The Philosophy of Management* (Pitman 1923)
12   F.J. Roethlisberger and W.J. Dickson, *Management and the Worker* (Harvard University Press 1939)
13   See: A. Cubbon, 'Hawthorne talk in context' *Occupational Psychology*, **43** (1969), pp. 111–28
     A. Carey, 'The Hawthorne Studies: A radical criticism', *American Sociological Review*, vol. 32, no. 3 (June 1967), pp. 403–16
     J. Shepard, 'On Alex Carey's radical criticism of the Hawthorne Studies', *Academy of Management Journal*, vol. 14, no. 1 (March 1971), pp. 23–32
14   J. E. Kelly, 'Understanding Taylorism: some comments', *British Journal of Sociology*, vol. 29, no. 2 (June 1978), p. 203
15   S. Huneryager and I. Heckmann, *Human Relations in Management* (2nd ed.) (South Western Publishing 1967), p. 1
16   T.S. Kuhn, *The Structure of Scientific Revolutions* (University of Chicago Press 1970)
17   J.K. Galbraith, *The Affluent Society* (Penguin 1962).
18   Institute of Marketing quoted in T. Cannon, *Basic Marketing* (Holt, Rinehart and Winston 1980)
19   P. Pigors and C. Myer *Personnel Administration* (6th ed.) (New York: McGraw-Hill 1969)
20   J. Lerner, *Introduction to Business Organisation and Management* (McGraw-Hill 1982)
21   H. Ansoff, *Corporate Strategy* (Penguin 1968), p. 17
22   J. O'Shaughnessy, *Patterns of Business Organisation* (George Allen and Unwin 1976), p. 185
23   A. Berle and S. Means, *The Modern Corporation and Private Property* (New York: Macmillan 1933)
24   J. Child, *The Business Enterprise in Modern Industrial Society* (Collier-Macmillan 1969).

2

CONTINGENCY THEORY AND POLITICS

Before we can understand people in organizations we must understand organizations themselves. In this chapter we continue our explorations into organization theory. The 'Contingency' approach is presented as a development of the systems model and the 'Strategic Choice' critique is used to provide the link to the political model which underlies this book.

The contingency approach to understanding organizations

In Chapter 1 we outlined the basic ideas of the influential open systems model of organizations. We noted its emphasis on relationships between the organization and its environment. This is a useful way of thinking which can help to identify key issues for managers when trying to cope with problems such as falling sales, new technology and new products. It provides insights for those who wish to design and manage organizations towards given goals. Our critique of the model so far has been based on managerialism; the model is, however, unsatisfactory in another important respect. It is a very broad model which, in essence, tells the manager he must consider the relationships between everything and everything else without offering guidance on specific problems. The contingency approach is a logical development from systems which overcomes this deficiency. It is basically the application of the same philosophy to individual aspects of management. Most contingency writers have focused on how to design the structure of the organization[1] but others have looked at leadership,[2] motivation,[3] hours systems[4] and even management accounting systems.[5] Why is it called 'contingency' theory? Because when looking at some aspect of organization these writers are concerned to discover the factors upon which its design should be based, that is upon which it is contingent.

Paul R. Lawrence and Jay W. Lorsch first used the term 'contingency theory' in their book *Organization and Environment*.[6] They aimed at a theory, based on systems concepts, which stressed the relevance of theory to practice in specific situations. Thus contingency theory aims to be useful both conceptually and

A rethink: Management researchers

Research is not an objective activity. The very questions the researcher chooses to ask, the variables he chooses to measure, the way he designs his study, the subjects he chooses to analyse and the conclusions he decides to draw, will all be influenced by his values and beliefs.

In the management field, researchers tend to be the products of management degrees and have been conditioned to a managerialist bias, or they come from other disciplines and tend to accept the conventional view in what is, for them, a new field.

These researchers often need access to organizations in order to obtain data; they are more likely to be accepted if their research is within the prevailing ethic. Few organizations will allow someone to look at their political processes and conflicts; many will be keen to help someone find ways to get more effort out of workers or more profits out of factories.

Researchers also may have other ambitions than furthering the bounds of knowledge. They may wish to write books, run courses and earn fame and fortune from their endeavours. They may believe they are more likely to be successful if their theories and conclusions are acceptable within the managerialist view.

The writers of this book are convinced this is not always the case!

operationally. In the first part of this chapter we shall be assessing how well it succeeds.

Kast and Rosenzweig state the central theme as follows:

'The contingency view of organizations and their management suggests that an organisation is a system composed of subsystems and delineated by identifiable boundaries from its environmental suprasystem. The contingency view seeks to understand the interrelationships within and among subsystems as well as between the organisation and its environment and to define patterns of relationships or configurations of variables. It emphasises the multivariate nature of organisations and attempts to understand how organisations operate under varying conditions and in specific circumstances.'[7]

Greenwood *et al* offer a simpler statement of the basic model:

'Contingency theory rests upon the assumption that organisational characteristics have to be shaped to meet situational circumstances. The extent to which any organisation secures a 'goodness of fit' between situational characteristics and structural characteristics will determine the level of organisational performance.'[8]

Contingency theorists assume that no single form of organization is universally applicable and hence their aims are to find relationships between particular 'contingency factors' and organizational characteristics, and ultimately to suggest *organizational designs* and *managerial practices* which are most appropriate for specific situations. This larger aim necessitates that a third set of variables be introduced, that is 'criteria of performance'.

Just as we have attempted to portray all previous organization theories in diagrammatic form, so Figure 4 is a simple representation of the contingency approach.

The general pattern of a piece of contingency research is as follows. Some aspect of organization is chosen about which managers need information:

What leadership style should we adopt?
What decision-making method should we use?
How many levels should there be in the hierarchy?

The researcher then studies a number of organizations and attempts to identify the key contextual variable(s) which relate to the organizational variable(s). Thus, in the case of leadership style, the key contextual variables may be the level of job involvement of employees, the experience of the supervisor, and the nature of the task. The researcher, from this analysis, will have a picture of the ways in which organizational and contextual factors are found together in actual organizations. He will then go on to look at the *effects* of these different combinations in terms of

Figure 4 *The contingency approaches to understanding organizations*

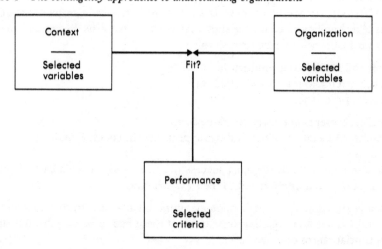

some criteria of performance. In terms of leadership style these might take forms such as output levels, absenteeism and morale.

From an analysis of the full results the researcher will then try to specify, *for a particular context*, what is most appropriate or the 'best fit' in terms of the organizational variable. In our example he may find that a very autocratic style achieves highest output with uncommitted workers on routine tasks, whereas a more democratic style works well with more highly motivated workers on less predictable tasks.

Let us now look at some examples of contingency studies.

Structure, technology and performance

Woodward's contingency study of the relationship between organization structure, technology and performance is one of the classic pieces of organizational research.[9] In essence it was simple enough but its impact has had a formative effect on much later work, particularly in the UK.

In the mid-1950s, a survey was conducted of 100 firms employing over 100 employees in south-east Essex. Woodward was concerned to know whether the most successful firms would be those whose structure most complied with the classical ideas outlined in Chapter 1. She obtained a great deal of background information about each company; its size, its industry, and its performance. Structure was measured in terms of three main variables:

1   The number of levels of authority in the management hierarchy
2   The average numbers of people reporting to each first line supervisor (span of control)
3   The ratio of managers and supervisory staff to other personnel (administrative component)

There were wide variations in structure which could not be related immediately to size, type, industry or effectiveness. It was not until firms were grouped according to their technological characteristics that distinct patterns began to emerge. Woodward categorized each firm simply as:

> Unit and small batch production
> Large batch and mass production, or
> Process production

Figure 5 represents her research framework.

Woodward's analysis of her findings approaches the conclusion that technology *determines* structure.

She also believed that the most successful firms using a particular technology were those which approximated to the *right* structure:

> 'It appeared that different technologies imposed different kinds of demands on individuals and organisations, and that these had to be met through an appropriate form of organisation.'

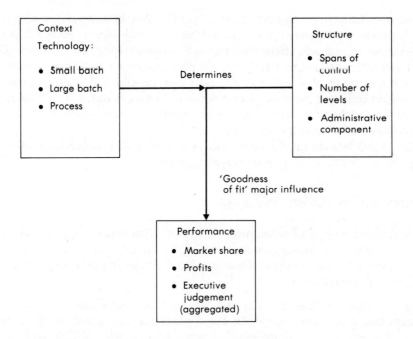

Figure 5 *John Woodward (1958)*

The 'right' structure was one which approximated to the average for all the firms with similar technology – since it was firms with structures of this configuration which turned out to be the high performers. Some other results are summarized in Table 1.

Thus a manager in a mass production firm employing 900 people might infer from Woodward's study that he should have between forty-one and fifty people, on average, reporting to each first line supervisor, four levels of authority in the hierarchy, and overall one manager or supervisor to every fifteen other employees.

Table 1 *Some of Woodward's results*

	Most successful firms		
	Average spans of control	Levels of authority	Admin. component No.of employees
Unit production	21–30	3	400– 500 = 22:1
			850–1000 = 37:1
			3000–4500 = 25:1
Mass production	41–50	4	400– 500 = 14:1
			850–1000 = 15:1
			3000–4500 = 18:1
Process production	11–20	6	400– 500 = 8.1
			850–1000 = 7:1
			3000–4500 = 7:1

Many criticisms can be made of Woodward's work, in terms of the research methods, the measurement processes and the findings.[10] Nevertheless it is clear that she has undermined classical principles by demonstrating that there is no one best structure for all situations. She has also provided a reminder to human relations theorists that effectiveness does not depend solely on individual motivation and group processes. Her major contribution, however, is undoubtedly in the form of the contingency framework underlying her research, upon which many later studies have been founded.

Let us now look at a more sophisticated contingency study which has profound implications for those who would shape organizations.

Organization and environment

Lawrence and Lorsch's fundamental question is 'What kind of organization does it take to deal with various economic and market conditions?'[11] They introduce two key variables into the study of management which are important aspects of the design of all organizations:

Differentiation Defined as 'The state of segmentation of the organizational system into subsystems' (p. 3). In other words the nature and degree of the breakdown of the organization into functions, departments and other units. For example, a company with low differentiation may not have a personnel department, all this type of work being distributed amongst line managers. On the other hand, a company with high differentiation may have not only a personnel department but may have within it specialists in recruitment, training, industrial relations, and so on.

Integration Defined both as 'The *process* of achieving unity of effort among the various subsystems in the accomplishment of the organization's task' (p. 4) and as 'The *quality* of the state of collaboration that exists among departments that are required to achieve unity of effort by the demands of the environment' (p. 11).

Thus it is the binding together of the different parts of the organization. Companies use a range of integrative methods.

The authority hierarchy is a simple integrative device. Paper controls such as job descriptions, procedures, rules, policy manuals and systems can all be effective. Direct supervision can be another simple mechanism.

More elaborate methods involve exchanges of personnel between departments, liaison officers, communication meetings, permanent interdepartmental teams or task forces for specific projects, and of course joint committees. Sometimes there are permanent managers or even departments performing integrative functions.

It should be noted that differentiation and integration are not simply structural concepts. They are also related to the attitudes of managers within the organization to each other and to the firm. To what extent do they feel part of a united enterprise pulling together? To what extent are they pursuing personal or departmental goals?

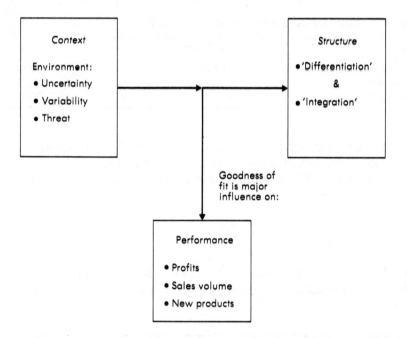

Figure 6 *Lawrence and Lorsch (1967)*

Lawrence and Lorsch conducted a number of studies but we shall outline just one, their research into three industries – plastics, food packaging and containers. They identified two firms in each industry, one a 'high performer' and one a 'low performer', in terms of profits, sales and new product innovation, and analysed the state of differentiation and integration which existed in each. Figure 6 represents their study.

Lawrence and Lorsch believed that the degree of differentiation and integration between departments within each firm should be related to the nature of the firm's environment. In the plastics industry they categorized the environment as 'highly uncertain', involving as it did in the 1960s fierce competition, short product life-cycles and rapidly changing technology. In the container industry there had been no major new products for two decades; average sales growth had kept pace with population growth but no more. Competition was predictable and not threatening; this was an environment of 'low uncertainty'. Somewhere in between ('moderate uncertainty') came food packaging. There was considerable innovation, but both new product generation and sales growth were lower than plastics and higher than containers. The *successful* firms in each industry followed the pattern shown in Table 2.

Differentiation was thus found to vary directly with environment, increasing as it became more complex, changeable and threatening.

Integration, on the other hand, always needed to be high. What changed, in this case, was the nature of the integrative devices – they became more elaborate and

Table 2   *Lawrence and Lorsch: Summary of results*

	Differentiation	Integration
Plastics	High	High
Food packaging	Moderate	High
Containers	Low	High

sophisticated as differentiation increased. Lawrence and Lorsch discovered that to have high differentiation and high integration at the same time is difficult and tends to lead to conflict within the organization. This creates a need for special integrative methods.

Hours systems

The work of Lee and McEwan Young[12] is a recent example of how contingency studies can be designed to aid managerial decision-making. The particular focus

---

A rethink: Context, organization and performance

Contingency studies of the ways in which organizational variables such as structure are related to the context and the performance of organizations often produce significant statistical relationships.

As a manager, however, I am unlikely to respond to the fact that most successful firms in my industry have a particular structure *unless it will benefit me* to make the recommended changes – even if I agree with the managerialist criteria of performance used in most studies.

Let us assume that I am a marketing manager and Lawrence and Lorsch's research has led me to believe that the organization requires fundamental changes – specifically, better liaison between marketing and production. I now have the problem of convincing my superior, the marketing executive, and then *we* must convince the managing director and production executive. But suppose the two executives are currently competing for the managing director's position when he retires next year? This may make matters difficult.

'Why should I bother?' If my boss is the one who becomes managing director, I may be considered for his job, particularly if I have been noticed because of my instigating a successful reorganization. But what if the changes have negative effects . . .?

of their studies has been the hours systems to which employees are subject. In essence they ask 'What degrees and forms of flexibility should be built into hours control systems in the pursuit of specific objectives under different circumstances?'

Despite the widespread use of different hours systems such as 'staggered hours', 'flexitime' and 'flexible rostering' in the last decade, managements still tend to adopt new systems without considering all the alternatives and their different effects. The researchers have produced a contingency framework for making this decision and have drawn on their own and others' research to analyse the relationships between the variables. Their framework is represented in a simplified form in Figure 7.

The organizational profile on the left hand side includes both the objectives which a management may choose to pursue and the organizational characteristics which influence the type of hours system that is appropriate. These include technological characteristics such as interdependence of workers and fluctuations in output requirements, as well as human and industrial relations considerations.

On the right hand side are the different types of hours control systems.

Without unnecessarily exploring the details of their study we shall note the underlying proposition – by considering the full range of hours systems, and the relationships between them and organizational characteristics, it is suggested that objectives are most likely to be achieved if a 'best fit' system can be identified.

Lee and McEwan Young differ from the other contingency writers we have

Figure 7   *Lee and McEwan Young (1977)*

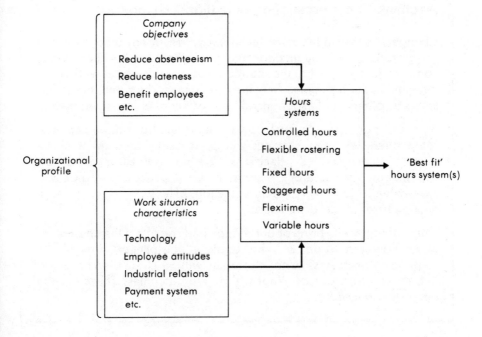

studied in that they take objectives to be variable. Nevertheless the ten 'company objectives' they analyse are distinctly managerialist. A recent paper by Lee[13] acknowledges this limitation and shows how far the reality of decisions over hours deviates from the contingency prescription. He describes the decision process at one company in which, despite a working party report strongly in favour of flexitime, and majority support amongst both employees and managers, the idea is finally dropped due to objections from some powerful managers.

Analysis of contingency theory

The contingency approach has been arguably the most influential input to organization theory in the last decade. For example, in the next chapter it is shown to underlie much modern research into leadership. It has led to many useful studies, such as those we have outlined, which have contributed greatly to the understanding and management of organizations. As with all theories in the social sciences, however, it has its limitations; by identifying them we will help to show the need for a political perspective.

Referring once again to Figure 4, the contingency theorist aims to study some key organizational variable or variables which it is important for managers to know about. He seeks to identify the major contextual influences on that variable (the

---

A rethink: The process of organizational change

Changes, be they in structure, technology, size, or any other aspect of organization, are brought about by people. Pressures for change may come from any aspect of the situation, but these pressures will always operate through people. They may be ignored by some, misunderstood by others, and experienced in a variety of different ways.

Sometimes groups with much power will bring about major changes. More often, however, changes will come about as a result of the accumulation of 'small' decisions. A supervisor takes on a new subordinate, a secretary resigns, a word processor replaces a typewriter, a manager restructures the jobs of his three foremen. Much change takes place incrementally.

Every manager can bring about change and can affect the attempts of other managers to do so. What goals will he pursue? How will he respond to pressures? What strategies will he choose? What interactions will take place? What will be the outcomes? These are the interesting questions.

factors upon which its impact is contingent) and then to analyse the effects of certain context/variable relationships. Already we can see some obvious methodological problems:

- The selection of key contextual factors is difficult; are we sure they are relevant?

- How do we *measure* organizational, contextual and performance variables?

- What do any statistical relationships between the variables really mean?

There are also problems from the practising manager's point of view. If he reads a contingency study which implies that in his context a different organization structure gives better results, how should he react? The sample sizes are often small, the measurement of variables is often dubious and the relationships are never certain. It is clear that no manager would take action on the basis of this evidence alone. He would want to know not only *what* relationships exist but *why*. This information cannot be found in contingency analysis; it requires insight into the *processes* of change which lead to the relationships in the first place. The processes of change inevitably involve political interaction, people trying to get their own way, conflict.

Strategic choice by dominant coalitions

One of the most influential critiques of contingency research as represented in Figure 4, comes from John Child.[14] He has argued that Woodward, Lawrence and Lorsch and others have attempted 'to explain organization at one remove by ignoring the essentially political process, whereby power-holders within organizations decide upon courses of strategic action' (p.1).

Child's basic model is shown in Figure 8.

Child uses, in his argument, the concept of the 'dominant coalition'. By this is usually meant the senior executive and directors of a company who often have a considerable influence over decisions and changes which occur. They create rules, policies, systems and procedures to help ensure that other employees behave in line with their wishes.

It is useful sometimes to refer to a dominant coalition at the top of the hierarchy. Certainly much power is centred there. Major decisions about, for instance, opening new factories, developing new markets and perhaps restructuring the hierarchy itself are often made at this level. The danger inherent in this idea, however, is that we forget that power is widely distributed throughout the organization. The 'strategic choice' critique points out weaknesses in many contingency studies:

- *People* make organizations, they are not determined by context. Power-holders may choose to oppose or ignore contextual influences. A manager may adopt a particular leadership style or design a particular structure for his department irrespective of their effect on profits or productivity.

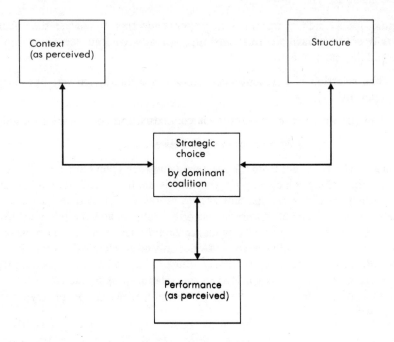

Figure 8   *A 'strategic contingencies' framework*

- *People* choose their own criteria of performance – which may not mean profits – they may mean a quiet life, or departmental rather than organizational efficiency.

- *People* may be able to choose and manipulate their own context, for example entering new markets, making new products or even influencing the passing of laws and government economic policy

These are sound comments but where we have written *people* it is not possible to write 'the dominant coalition'.

Once we start to 'open up' the decision-making process (see Chapters 6 to 9), it becomes clear that the idea of a dominant coalition, however much it is hedged, still implies an oversimple view of reality. It is not enough to talk of 'strategic choice' and focus on one, or a few, powerful groups. We must study the political situation and political activity, and accept that there will be many interest groups influencing structure (and other organizational variables) as they push towards their own goals. They will make their own political choices on the basis of their own political analyses of the situation, and outcomes will depend on the complex interactions which take place.

So what is the value of contingency research studies? Essentially they are useful because they tell us about the broad relationships between variables which processual studies must explain. They help us to identify testable hypotheses for the processual researcher – such as:

A rethink: The dominant coalition

The idea of a 'dominant coalition' which has considerable power to affect most major aspects of the organization's structure and systems, and to affect the course of events, is dangerously convenient to the writer on organizational politics.

It is true that at a certain high level in the hierarchy, perhaps at the board of directors level, there is a considerable concentration of power. Decisions taken at this level include those which are commonly known as 'organizational policy'. It is also there that rules, regulations, procedures and major changes of direction are often initiated or approved. Compliance with these directives is encouraged by the use of control, reward and sanction systems such as budgets, appraisal, promotion, and pay.

The concept of a dominant coalition is dangerous however, on a number of grounds. Unity among senior managers is rare. These people are successful political animals, more used than most to being right and getting their way. They are often ambitious and competitive. Hence the coalition will be divided for many if not most purposes. Also it is not an easy matter for managers at this level to gain information and implement decisions. They rely on others to write reports, prepare analyses and take action. This makes them vulnerable to skilful political tactics from those below them and may also mean they must moderate plans to obtain co-operation.

It is not possible to simply postulate the concept of a dominant coalition and then proceed as though the other internal and external influences on organizational behaviour were insignificant. This is true whatever the advantages of simplification. The inaccuracies involved are as great as the flaws in the classical model of organization theory.

- For effective performance, in a firm with small or unit batch production there should be average spans of control of 21–30. (Woodward)
  and

- For effective performance, firms in highly changeable and threatening environments should have high differentiations and high integration using elaborate integrative mechanisms. (Lawrence and Lorsch)

By examining structural change while it is actually happening and by analysing the decisions made by the parties concerned, we may find explanations for the contingency conclusions. We may also hope to find explanations for the exceptions to the rule. This will make the understandably wary manager much more confident about making changes. He must remember, however, that even if *he* is convinced of the need for change in the pursuit of what *he* sees as desirable goals, he may still have problems in persuading others. Making changes is often a complex political process; just knowing what you want to do does not make it happen.

The new direction

A company had argued persuasively to its employees for years that they did not need a union. They paid higher wages than the unionized company nearby and offered better working conditions. Everyone was happy until the redundancies were announced, then the employees had no voice.

The work study manager of a manufacturing company discovered that if he appointed difficult shop stewards to be work study engineers they ceased to cause trouble. Furthermore they were aware of the dodges used by their former colleagues and this made them much better at their task.

A young office clerk saw that the new computer was causing problems for her manager. She resolved to learn everything about it and make herself valuable. Within a year the manager was totally reliant on her; she had received an upgrading and a merit rise.

These short examples from our experience cannot be neatly explained by any of the organization theories so far examined. There can be few managers who could not bring a dozen such cases to mind. They are just commonplace manifestations of a simple fact – in most organizations everybody is not pulling in the same direction. The idea of the firm as a neat 'system' characterized by co-operation and teamwork is not always a true reflection of reality. If we accept that there are both sectional and individual interests within an organization, and see the interactions of interest groups as the key to understanding, then we have the beginnings of a political model.

Politics and managerialism

Consider the following definitions:

'Company politics is the *byplay* that occurs when people want to advance themselves or their ideas regardless of whether or not these ideas would *help the company*.' E. Hegarty [15]

'Political manoeuvering refers to actions that are directed more toward self-aggrandizement than toward the good of the company as a whole. Playing politics connotes a degree of deception and dishonesty.' A. Dubrin [16]

'Politics are the exploitation of resources, both physical and human, for the achievement of more control over others, and thus of safer, or more comfortable, or more satisfying terms of existence.' T. Burns [17]

'Political behaviour is defined as behaviour by individuals, or, in collective terms, by sub-units, within an organization that makes a claim against the resource-sharing system of the organization.' A. Pettigrew [18]

'Politics: any behaviour that is self-serving.' S. Robbins [19]

To the first two writers organizational politics is clearly undesirable. It is not the usual behaviour of the average individual but a particular kind of activity which is indulged in from time to time by those who wish to subvert the way things should be done. Politics is deviation rather than normality. These writers are 'Political Managerialists'. They accept that all is not neat and tidy, that the organization is not a goal-directed network of systems. They accept that individuals do not all work towards the goals of the organization. Their view, however, is that organizations do, or should, have goals and their members should work towards them. The pursuit of personal goals to the detriment of organizational goals constitutes political behaviour.

This political managerialist model encourages the identification of ways of avoiding, or overcoming, any deviation from 'organization goals'. It places the writer squarely on the side of one particular interest group and leads him to be critical of contrary views.

The other definitions, those of Burns, Pettigrew and Robbins, however, adopt no managerialist perspective. They make no assumptions about organizational goals and do not automatically accept the rights of any 'dominant coalition' to specify how people should behave. This perspective, which we might call the 'Radical Political' view, does not encourage discussion of rights and wrongs, deviations or dysfunctions. It characterizes the organization in terms of different individuals and interest groups who will try to get their own way to the best of their ability. No single interest group – such as owners, managers or trade unions – is given by the observer any special right to influence organizational activity, although the groups may accord such rights to each other. Adopting the radical view avoids questions such as:

Who says what the organization's goals should be?
What if there is no agreement within this group?
What if other groups disagree?
Where does this group get the right to set goals?
What rights do other groups have?

By this view, even the board of directors is merely another interest group pursuing its own goals to the best of its ability. It is the radical political perspective which provides the conceptual basis for this book.

The radical political perspective
It is clear that a business organization will normally consist of people, land, buildings, machinery, materials, work methods, rules and procedures, money,

products and a host of other paraphernalia aggregated together. At the same time this is an inadequate description of the business organization, and in the theories examined so far we have outlined a number of attempts to improve on it. Each of these attempts, each organization theory, focuses on particular variables and their interrelationships. Again we have discussed our view of each of these theories in terms of the insights it offers. It is already clear to the reader that, whilst recognizing that all have value, the perspective we favour for the study of organizational behaviour is a political one. In the remainder of this chapter we will clarify the precise nature of the political perspective underlying all the succeeding chapters.

Reification

Some approaches reify the business organization by positing that it behaves or pursues objectives in some unitary way, independently of the people who work within it. Our political model does not do this. It is, for us, self-evident that the form the business organization takes, and the activities which relate to it, are both the result of human activity, including the sometimes wilful and self-seeking activity of particular individuals or internal groups.

Managerialism

Similarly, our model is not based on the managerialist assumption that organizations have, or should have, goals which management has the right to decide. For us no interest group has any *a priori* rights, although we accept that they might be assumed to have, either by themselves or by other parties (and this may affect the situation politically). Also, in our model, it is not useful to judge any set of values or beliefs as 'right' or 'wrong'.

The business organization consists fundamentally of individuals. These individuals form a large 'uneasy coalition'. The 'uneasiness' results from the personal behaviour pattern of each individual, which is a consequence of his personal interests, beliefs, values and goals, as well as his response to his environment and his contact with other people. Frequently individuals come together to form smaller 'uneasy coalitions' within the business organization. These in turn may engage in behaviour patterns which are intended to help the group in its pursuit of its own goals.

From this it is clear that in our model the individual is characterized as essentially rational and active in the pursuit of his personal goals. The idea that the individual is primarily irrational, emotional, or a passive responder to internal needs or drives – a view which is implicit in many theories of organizational behaviour – is rejected here. Nevertheless it is an important part of our model to acknowledge that people are often constrained to pursue the goals of others, and that personal goals (and the values and beliefs underlying them) may also be modified as the result of the will and power of others. Some of these ideas on motivation are developed further in Chapter 3.

Because different organizational members are pursuing ends which are often to some degree incompatible, conflict is likely to occur. This is a natural consequence and is not usefully regarded as 'bad'. The usual outcome of conflict is either its continuation in a different form or some sort of resolution. On the other hand, many forms of conflict can continue indefinitely without threatening the organization's survival.

The processes of conflict, political activity and conflict resolution are characteristic activities of organizational life, and typically result in a state of dynamic equilibrium. Compromises are common because most members of the business organization share an interest in its survival.

The nature of the conflict resolution will tend to favour those with most power. Power is thus the central variable in our political perspective, and it may be simply defined, at this stage, as the ability to affect outcomes. (See Chapters 6, 7, 8 and 9.)

History, structure and context

So far we have not developed any explanation for the fact that power is unevenly distributed within business organizations. Different individuals and groups have different abilities to affect different types of outcome, depending on a wide range of factors, chief amongst which are often position in the hierarchy, membership of particular interest groups, and access to scarce resources.

Thus there is an existing political structure which has evolved over time as a result of political activity and which results in differences in ability to influence organizational outcomes. In general we see a concentration of this ability at the top of the hierarchy. The hierarchy itself is an important part of the political structure.

The mere fact of a position near the top of the hierarchy does not, however, guarantee dominant power in any particular organizational situation. Furthermore the idea of a single interest group or 'dominant coalition' at the top is too simple. Those at the top may not form a cohesive interest group, or their own conflicts may lead to ambiguity in their use of power. Furthermore they may be affected by information fed to them by lower levels in the hierarchy which has been filtered in order to influence their response. And there are many other political counter-balances which offset the power of those in top positions.

The concentration of power at the top of the hierarchy is a distinctive feature of business organizations, but for our purposes we do not judge it as right to treat the goals of those who are at the top as those of the organization. They are simply one particular interest group pursuing their own goals with the power at their command.

Figure 9 represents the major actors in our political perspective. The forces which flow between them cannot easily be represented.

It will be noted, particularly from the diagrammatic representation of the political view, that we do not confine our considerations to internal interest groups. There is a wide range of external actors, including the government, customers, competitors, suppliers, shareholders, distributors and others, all trying to influence organizational activity.

Neither is the context of the organization confined to actors. There are also the laws, the economy, the culture and other features of the society in which it exists. These aspects of the context, like the structure of the organization, have been

A rethink: Induction, selection, training, appraisal, budget, expenditure, scheduling and other systems

Most organizations are permeated by a complex network of systems. These have a very significant effect on events and activities within the organization. They are designed to encourage certain types of behaviour and discourage others; often they are related to reward and sanction systems. It is usually hard for an individual to achieve his basic goals without at least appearing to comply with these controls.

Thus there is considerable power in being part of the systems – providing information and 'enforcing' rather than merely being 'subject to'.

There is even more power in being able to design the systems and specify the goals they will be created to pursue.

The creation of systems is normally controlled from high up the hierarchy and helps to justify the term 'dominant coalition' for those who work there. We should note, however, that systems are applied, and information is fed to them, at lower levels of the hierarchy. This provides considerable opportunity for political activity which is not intended by the system creators.

shaped by the political activities of past generations. We should note, however, that just as structure can be changed by current actions so can external contexts often be changed, either directly or by avoidance. Business organizations are not always tied to particular products, markets or even countries.

The people within the organization are affected by its context, as well as by their perceptions of how they should behave. Their values and their goals have all been moulded, to some extent, by the world in which they were raised and have to survive. In other words, we conceptualize man as a rational actor but we are aware of the factors which affect his deliberations.

Conclusions

To summarize, in this section we have outlined the essence of our political model of organizations. It involves no reification of the organization as though it were a person who could think, have goals and take action. It involves no managerialist assumptions about management prerogatives and obligations. The individual is characterized as active and essentially rational in the pursuit of his goals. The organization is characterized as a complex network of competing and co-operating individuals and coalitions in which conflict is a natural occurrence. The central

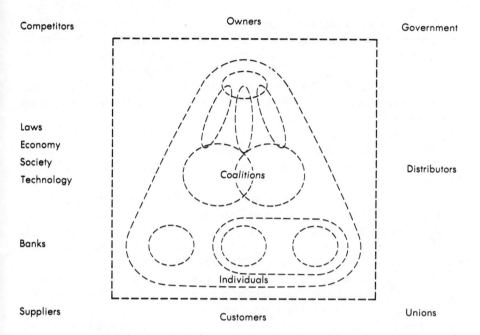

Figure 9   *The main political actors*

variable of the political model is power, and understanding of its nature and consequences is essential if the mysteries of the organization are to be unravelled. Skill in its use is essential for personal achievement. Political insight requires knowledge of external as well as internal factors. We also need to note the importance of past political activity in creating much of the context for, and thus affecting the nature of, current behaviour.

Organization theory and OB

In these first two chapters we have outlined the development of the main organization theories which have influenced OB. A knowledge of organization theory is important because without it we cannot give any perspective to the specific study of people in organizations. If we do not know what the organization is doing, what the key variables are that describe it, and what binds it together to make it an 'organization', then how can we interpret the behaviour of people within it? It would be like trying to tell how large an item is when it is drawn alone on a piece of paper. With no framework to fit it into, with no possible comparisons, how can we guess?

Experience by itself is useless. It has to be learned from by extracting the key lessons and identifying patterns of relationships – developing a theory. The more we make our personal organization theory explicit and submit it to the test of real life use, the more useful it will become.

Yet we have seen a range of different theories, each with their own strengths and weaknesses in particular situations. The classical ideas are a good starting point for thinking about organizations; their emphases on structure, the divorce of planning from doing, and 'money motivation' provide a reasonable first approximation to many business activities. The human relations approach introduces a much more sophisticated view of people to help us in direct interpersonal situations. Systems and contingency models are likely to appeal to the committed managerialist as prescriptions for what *should* happen in organizations. They also have an important political purpose as propaganda devices, for use in colleges and in companies, to persuade managers and future managers of the rightness of managerialist views.

Finally we have looked at the political perspective. This emerging school of thought offers some politically awkward, often unacceptable, ideas on the inevitability of conflict and the nature of power in organizations. It also, as we shall see, directs us at some new questions for OB. No longer do we just need to ask 'How should we design jobs to minimize decision-making?', 'How can we get people to work harder?', 'How can we make supervisors better leaders?' or 'How can we improve communications and decision-making?'. Now we must ask 'What are the ways in which people influence each other?', 'How do people formulate strategies?', 'How are changes made in organizations?'. Furthermore we must ask these questions not to make organizations more efficient in the managerialist sense; *our* purpose is to provide insights which will help *any* organizational member in the pursuit of his or her goals – whatever they may be.

References

1   The classic studies are:
    J. Woodward, *Management and Technology* (HMSO 1958)
    P.R. Lawrence and J.W. Lorsch, *Organisation and Environment* (Harvard Graduate School of Business Administration 1967)
    T. Burns and G.M. Stalker, *The Management of Innovation* (Social Science Paperbacks 1961)
    D.S. Pugh and D.J. Hickson *Organizational Structure in its Context* (Saxon House 1976)
2   F.E. Fiedler, 'How do you make leaders more effective? New answers to an old puzzle', *Organisational Dynamics* (Autumn 1972), pp. 3–18
3   J.J. Morse and J.W. Lorsch, 'Beyond Theory Y', *Harvard Business Review* (May–June 1970), pp. 61–68
4   R.A. Lee and W. McEwan Young, 'A contingency approach to work week structuring', *Personnel Review*, vol. 6, no. 2 (Spring 1977), pp. 46–55
5   J.H. Waterhouse and P. Tiessen, 'A contingency framework for management accounting systems research', *Accounting Organizations and Society*, vol. 3, no. 1 (1978), pp. 65–76
6   *ibid.*
7   F.E. Kast and J.E. Rosenzweig, *Contingency Views of Organization and Management* (New York: Science Research Associates 1973)

8   R. Greenwood, C.R. Hinings and S. Ranson, 'Contingency theory and the organisation of Local Authorities', Part 1, *Public Administration* (Spring 1975), p. 2

9   Woodward, *Management and Technology*

10 L. Donaldson, 'Woodward, technology, organization structure, and performance – a critique of the universal generalization', *Journal of Management Studies*, vol. 13, no. 3 (October 1976), pp. 255–73.

11 *ibid.*

12 *ibid.*

13 R.A. Lee, 'Recent trends in the managerial use of flexible working hours', *Personnel Review*, vol. 9, no. 3 (Summer 1980), pp. 51–53

14 J. Child, 'Organizational structure, environment and performance: the role of strategic choice', *Sociology*, vol. 6 (1972), pp. 1–22

15 E. Hegarty, *How to Succeed in Company Politics* (New York: McGraw-Hill 1976)

16 A. Dubrin, *Fundamentals of Organisational Behaviour* (New York: Pergamon Press 1978)

17 T. Burns, 'Micropolitics: mechanisms of institutional change', *Administrative Science Quarterly*, vol. 6, no. 3 (1961), pp. 257–81

18 A. Pettigrew, 'Towards a political theory of organizational intervention', *Human Relations*, vol. 28, no. 3 (1975), pp. 191–208

19 S. Robbins, *Organisational Behavior: Concepts and Controversies* (Englewood Cliffs, NJ: Prentice Hall 1979)

Part Two ━━━━━━━━━━━

DEVELOPMENTS IN ORGANIZATIONAL BEHAVIOUR

The reader is now aware of the organization theories which underlie much of conventional OB and their major assumptions. He or she is also aware of our critique of these theories and the political framework which has guided it and which led to the writing of this book.

In the next three chapters we outline the basic theories of some of the major aspects of conventional OB - motivation, group dynamics, and organization structures, cultures and climates. OB is a wider field than this, but by concentrating on three of its most developed topics we can introduce the reader to a substantial proportion of the subject and show how the political view creates new interpretations and challenges for those who study and manage organizations.

3

THE MOTIVES
OF PEOPLE

In this chapter we explore the most written about aspect of OB – motivation. The related subject of leadership is included as an important development from early motivation theories. A range of approaches to motivation and leadership is outlined, and then discussed in the light of our political perspective. The political model of human behaviour which underlies later chapters is developed.

Motivation

From an OB perspective, 'motivation' is the study of the driving forces which help to explain the individual's behaviour in the organization. 'Why do people work?' and 'How can we get people to work harder?' are the two most common questions in the literature. Most researchers have joined the managerialist quest to help managers persuade, encourage, cajole or manipulate their subordinates to perform tasks better for the good of the organization.

The goals of the person or group doing the motivating of others are rarely questioned. It is simply assumed that the committed manager is striving to increase efficiency and improve performance.

Within our model things are not so clear-cut. The manager may be trying to motivate his subordinates towards his own ends directly or, perhaps, towards what *he* sees as appropriate ends for the organization. Much behaviour in organizations is not simply about efficiency. Many things happen which are concerned with careers, satisfactions, socio/psychological games, conflicts and the full range of behavioural richness and diversity which makes life so interesting, challenging, stressful and rewarding. Is it not likely that the manager, or indeed any organization member, will try to 'motivate' others to help him achieve *whatever* ends he is pursuing? We shall return to this theme later but first let us review the development of motivation theories by examining those which are most well known.

A rethink: Theories of motivation

The theories of motivation covered in most books on OB are about understanding human motives and their relationship to efficient work behaviour. Their aim is to develop ideas, prescriptions, techniques, skills and awareness which will help supervisors to get the best performance out of subordinates. Thus the bias is strongly managerialist and this narrows their focus and range of application. In practice, most supervisors are concerned with 'how to get people to work harder' only as part of the broader question of 'how to get people to do what I want'. The broader question involves no managerialist bias and need not be restricted to supervisors. Thus motivation theories are really just a sub-set of theories of influence.

By focusing on this particular sub-set of ideas with their particular emphasis, most courses for managers and students are affecting the attitudes of the participants in a specific way. People are, in fact, being socialized into adopting managerialist beliefs. This may be an unspoken objective of many such courses. Those which are run for managers have to be justified to higher levels of the hierarchy. Those at colleges and universities have to satisfy the narrow views of professors and lecturers and perhaps the expectations of students who have already been socialized.

Paradoxically, the failure to study influence and recognize the political nature of organizations leads to many of the criticisms of OB as 'unrealistic' and 'unhelpful' to practising managers.

Classical ideas about motivation

In Chapter 1 the classical theory of organizations was reviewed. These successful managers and consultants, such as Taylor and Fayol, have tended to focus primarily on money, job design, discipline and supervision as the four most important influences on worker effort. None of them present a detailed theory of motivation, and it is later reviewers who have attributed ideas to them by 'reading between the lines' of their published work. Figure 10 summarizes their basic approach.

The generally accepted view is that the classical writers assumed the worker to conform to what McGregor later called 'Theory X'[1]:

'1   The average human being has an inherent dislike of work and will avoid it if he can.

2   Because of this human characteristic of dislike of work, most people must be coerced, controlled, directed, threatened with punishment to get

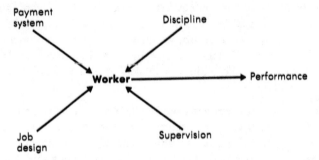

Figure 10   *Classical ideas about motivation*

them to put forth adequate effort toward the achievement of organizational objectives.

3   The average human being prefers to be directed, wishes to avoid responsibility, has relatively little ambition, wants security above all.'

Thus the worker is typified as money-motivated, idle and untrustworthy. This is in contrast to the manager who is seen as capable of taking responsibility, broadly motivated and fit to take charge.

The idea that people are motivated by money is inherently attractive to many students of management when they first think about motivation. After all, would not they work harder for more money? Is not that why they are keen to learn, so that eventually they can earn more?

Equally, for many practising managers, the money motivation argument is felt to be strong. After all, are not their subordinates always striving to earn more bonus and negotiate better pay rates?

There has been, as we shall see, strong reaction against these ideas. Much of it has gone too far, reducing the importance of money and emphasizing different motivators, on the basis of questionable data and theories. But the reader should consider the following points:

● Money may not always be a desirable motivator; it is expensive and may have only short-term effects. A pay rise may increase enthusiasm for a while but eventually it becomes just 'the rate for the job'.

● Money is often a means to an end, rather than an end in itself. If the real motivation is security or status, then perhaps these can be satisfied in other ways.

● If money is the only satisfaction a job provides then workers will inevitably be money-motivated.

● Often a manager does not have direct influence over his subordinates' wages but can influence other factors such as type of work, involvement and responsibility.

● Finally, for most of us, money *is* important but other rewards and satisfactions
   are important too. For example we might sacrifice promotion rather than
   leave a friendly work group; we might work very hard on a project that we
   think is worthwhile in its own right; or we might not work well for a supervisor
   whom we do not like. Money is thus only a part of the motivation picture for
   any individual.

In truth, few classical writers would make such crude assumptions as those of
Theory X if asked directly, and there has recently been a spirited defence of their
central ideas.[2] If output is the aim, their advice on incentive schemes, job
specialization and control of workers is undoubtedly of value. Nevertheless they
do oversimplify the issue of motivation, partly by overemphasizing the role of
money but mainly by seeing motivation as more a question of organization design
than supervisory skill.

In practice, the *motivational context*, which includes systems, structure and
culture of the organization, *is* a major factor but it interacts with the influences of
the *motivational relationships* in which the individual is involved. These are the
central focus of our second approach to motivation.

Early human relations ideas about motivation

As we saw in Chapter 1, from their research at Hawthorne and elsewhere, Elton
Mayo and other early human relations writers saw the significance of motivation as
a field of study. For them the organization's key variable is people and the quality
and quantity of their efforts are the major determinants of organizational success.
Edgar Schein sums up their assumptions about human nature:[33]

'1 Social needs are the prime motivator of human behaviour and
     interpersonal relationships the prime shaper of a sense of identity.
 2 As a result of the mechanization entailed in the Industrial Revolution,
     work has lost much of its intrinsic meaning, which now must be sought
     in social relationships on the job.
 3 Employees are more responsive to the social forces of the peer group
     than to the incentives and controls of management.
 4 Employees are responsive to management to the extent that a supervisor
     can meet a subordinate's needs for belonging, for acceptance, and for a
     sense of identity.'(P62)

This view of motivation is represented in Figure 11.
   The consequence of this approach to motivation was a dramatic expansion of
interest in the role of the supervisor. The onus for securing worker performance
was placed largely on his shoulders. He was encouraged to develop leadership
skills and learn about work group dynamics. F.J. Burns Morton provides an
example of this kind of exhortation:

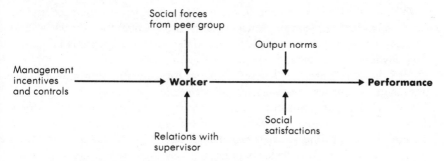

Figure 11   *Early human relations ideas about motivation*

'As a leader in the workshop the foreman should
(a)   weld the group together in a harmonious whole,
(b)   maintain authority as the democratic group,
(c)   encourage spontaneous discipline,
(d)   accept full responsibility for the group,
(e)   establish firm, fair, friendly treatment of employees,
(f)   raise morale, and create enthusiasm,
(g)   inspire security, certainty and confidence.'[4]

Thus for the early human relations writers the key to higher performance was *leadership skills* rather than incentive schemes or imposed discipline. Like motivation, the subject of leadership has expanded into a sub-discipline in its own right. At this stage we shall take a small detour to examine the development of these ideas.

Leadership

Classical writers tended to think of 'leadership' in terms of the qualities required of a good leader. The reader might be prepared to make generalizations: intelligence, confidence, initiative, popularity, vitality?

This focus on leadership *qualities* which are hard to measure, hard to validate and hard to change was superseded by the early human relations writers in favour of leadership *style*. They argued that the leader's *behaviour* is what the subordinate experiences directly, not his personal characteristics. Behaviour patterns have the advantage that they can be learned; the emphasis moved from selecting good leaders to training good leaders.

These first students of leadership asked the question 'How much direction should a leader give to his subordinates?' A continuum of possibilities was identified ranging from the highly 'autocratic' leader, who gave detailed instructions and expected unquestioning implementation, on the basis of his formal authority, to the extreme 'laissez-faire' leader, who abdicated from the work group and allowed subordinates to carry out self-selected tasks in their own way. At first, studies seemed to indicate that 'effective' leaders used the middle range 'democratic' leadership style which 'takes into consideration the wishes and suggestions of the members as well as those of the leader. It is a human relations approach where all members of the group are seen as important contributors to the final decision. Participation is sought to encourage member commitment to the decision and to improve the quality of the decision.'[5]

Gradually, however, researches began to show up problems with this widely acclaimed, but misnamed, democratic style. First came the realization that 'degree of direction' was only one way of categorizing leadership styles. A perhaps more helpful alternative method became popular; this classified leaders according to the extent to which they were:

1   task or production oriented, and
2   relationship or people oriented.

Task centred leaders:

> concentrate on getting the job done.
> assign tasks to subordinates.
> emphasize the importance of output and deadlines.
> expect routines and systems to be followed.
> stress being ahead of the competition.
> let subordinates know what is expected of them.

Relationship-centred leaders:

> are highly concerned with their relationships with subordinates.
> take time to get to know people. Listen.
> are friendly and approachable.
> help subordinates with personal problems.
> support subordinates to outside groups.

A number of writers have used this type of classification.[6] The best known of these are Blake and Mouton whose 'Managerial Grid' has been the inspiration of many later studies.

Concern for people and for production are not mutually exclusive, as a brief glance at the nature of task and relationship centred leaders will show. Blake and Mouton discuss the five styles shown in Figure 12. The 1,1 manager is seen as one who has withdrawn from the fray, leaving his subordinates to their own devices. The 1,9 manager has taken human relations ideas too much to heart; the 9,1 manager has perhaps taken classical ideas on the pursuit of efficiency to an extreme, without thought for social relationships.

For Blake and Mouton, the best managerial style is 9,9. This is the manager who realizes that a high concern for production can be coupled with a high concern for people. In fact these are often complementary qualities which can result in effectiveness beyond pure task centredness.

The second move away from the 'autocratic–democratic–laissez-faire' continuum can be summarized in the phrase 'horses for courses'. It became evident

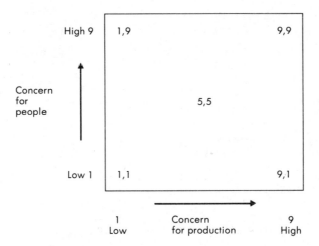

Figure 12   *The Blake and Mouton Managerial Grid*

from a large number of studies that there was no one best leadership style for all situations. The effective manager would have to tailor his approach to meet the prevailing circumstances. So what were the important factors in the situation and how were they related to leadership style and performance? The reader may recognize these as typical questions underlying the contingency framework described in Chapter 2.

The contingency theory of leadership is now the most popular approach and we can summarize the major work in one contingency diagram, see Figure 13. As with organization structure, different researchers have explored different variables.

Vroom and Yetton urge the leader to adopt different styles depending on the characteristics of the task. They argue that the leader has to consider the characteristics of each decision before deciding whether, and in what ways, to involve subordinates. 'Will the subordinates accept the decision if they are not involved?' 'Do I have sufficient information to decide alone?' 'Can subordinates be trusted to take into account organizational considerations?' These are among the primary questions. They provide a decision-tree to help with the process of defining the task-style relationships.

Fiedler believes that appropriate styles can be identified by considering particular situations in terms of their 'favourableness'. Favourableness is closely related to power. A 'favourable' situation from the leader's point of view is one in which tasks are highly structured, leader–member relationships are good and respect is high, and the leader has a high level of reward, and coercive and legitimate power. Such situations are, according to Fiedler, most suitable for task oriented leaders.

As favourableness reduces, so relationship oriented leaders do better, until, that is, the situation becomes very unfavourable. Under such unfavourable circumstances, Fiedler argues, the relationship oriented leader becomes unwilling to put

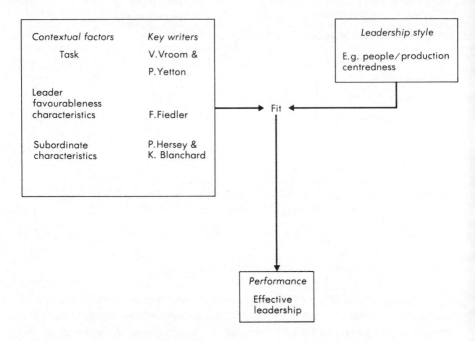

Figure 13   *Contingency theories of leadership*

any task pressures on subordinates. So at this point the task centred leader can do better by structuring the situation, for example with artificial deadlines or attendance rules or systems, thus reducing the ambiguity for subordinates.

On the other hand, two other researchers, Hersey and Blanchard, see the key dimension for determining leadership style as the 'maturity' of the subordinates. This is motivational maturity rather than advancing years. Their concept of maturity involves commitment to the task, and capacity to set appropriate self-goals and accept responsibility for their achievement.

When subordinate maturity is low, a task centred approach is recommended. As it increases, the leaders can also begin to develop relationships and hope to improve effectiveness further. Hersey and Blanchard see the role of the leader as not simply to respond to subordinates but also to take steps to increase their maturity – gradually encouraging, educating, involving and delegating until they begin to need less task supervision. Ultimately, for highly capable and mature subordinates it may be appropriate for the leader to have only a minimal level of interaction. This developmental process is represented in Figure 14.

These contingency approaches all identify some important feature which can influence the likelihood of success in leadership attempts. Since all situations are unique there can be no 'one best way' to lead, and theories which point this out and identify ways of analysing the problem are helpful. These theories also tend to be used as the bases for management training courses, so that the 'leader' can be taught useful diagnostic skills and behaviour patterns.

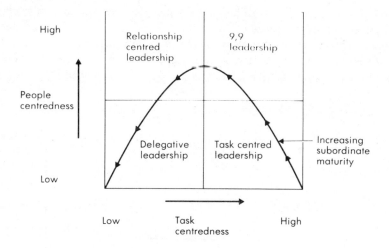

Figure 14   *Hersey and Blanchard's model of leadership*

We sidetracked slightly into this brief review of leadership from its beginnings in the work of Elton Mayo and his identification of the importance of work group – supervisor relationships. Now let us return to our original theme of motivation.

Later human relations ideas about motivation

A significant turning point in the theory of motivation occurred in the mid 1950s. Just as the Hawthorne Studies (see Chapter 1) had marked a major move away from classical ideas, so the ideas of Abraham Maslow[7] started a new era of sophistication in thinking about people. His theory is represented in Figure 15, juxtaposed against two more recent writers Herzberg[8] and Alderfer[9] who have developed his ideas.

For Maslow each individual has a hierarchy of needs which he tries to satisfy. It is the unsatisfied needs which motivate behaviour. Basically, the lower level needs are more powerful than those further up the hierarchy and will tend to take precedence. Thus a worker who is tired or hungry will take steps to satisfy those needs before he will be affected by needs for friendship and belonging (social needs) or respect, status and recognition (ego needs). The last category of needs to operate is that at the top of the hierarchy. Self-actualization is the need for self-fulfilment; it is the driving force which an individual perceives to be behind his existence. Maslow states that the satisfaction of this need can only be short-lived. Soon a new drive will emerge to influence the individual's behaviour.

There are a number of difficulties with Maslow's hierarchy of needs. First, it does not apply neatly to specific individuals. We can all cite examples of people who appear not to have needs for friendship or ego satisfaction. Often an ambitious manager will make himself unpopular to achieve advancement, sometimes he will

take considerable risks with his own financial security and he may even work to
physical and psychological exhaustion.

An equally difficult problem for the practising supervisor is that employees
often obtain need satisfaction outside of the work environment. Workers may be
most concerned with their friends or family at home and disinterested in work

Figure 15   *Need theories of motivation – Maslow's hierarchy*

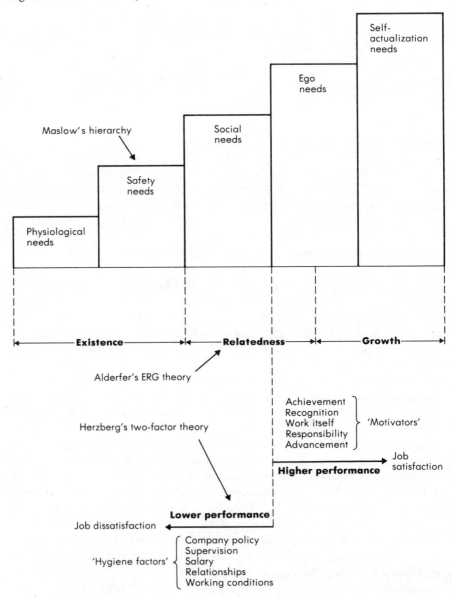

relationships. They may achieve ego satisfaction from running marathons, growing prize onions, or perhaps within the trade union movement.

Alderfer deals, at least in part, with these difficulties by postulating three main sets of needs, shown in Figure 15. 'Existence' needs are concerned with day-to-day survival; 'relatedness' needs are those based on interaction with others; 'growth' needs involve personal development and fulfilment. These are not arranged in a hierarchy and any of them may motivate an individual in different circumstances. Furthermore it is suggested that 'growth' needs, rather than being satisfied, may increase in intensity with achievement.

Herzberg asked people to talk about the things which caused changes in their level of job satisfaction. He then categorized the major factors which people said caused job satisfaction and job dissatisfaction, and weighted them according to the length of time they were talked about.

Herzberg discovered, as Figure 15 shows, that the factors which, when positive, lead to satisfaction do not, when negative, tend to lead to dissatisfaction. Conversely, the factors which, when negative, lead to dissatisfaction do not, when positive, tend to lead to satisfaction. Take pay, for example. When people perceive pay as too low it tends to make them feel dissatisfied. When it is perceived as high, however, it does not lead to particular satisfaction.

Herzberg called the dissatisfiers 'hygiene factors'. He saw these as the background conditions which should be satisfied for all employees in order to create fertile conditions for the satisfiers or 'motivators' to operate.

It may be noted that the hygiene factors refer primarily to the environment of work, whereas the motivators are related to the things people can at least try to influence themselves. This implies for management that promotion and training opportunities, and appraisal systems which provide feedback and recognition, are important motivators. It also throws particular emphasis on the way jobs are designed, and Herzberg saw this as a key area. He recommends 'job enrichment', building into the job factors such as variety, challenge, interest and responsibility. If possible, the enriched job should allow for the learning of new skills to cope with new problems. Most importantly, it should be 'open ended' in some way, to allow for taking on more responsibility and for changing and improving work methods.

These three related theories are useful because they provide a language for thinking about motivation. The different types of needs and the ways in which organizations and supervisors may facilitate their satisfaction are an important part of OB.

The problem from the practising manager's point of view is that he does not know which theory to follow and in any case they are difficult to put into practice. How, for example, is he to discover where an employee is on Maslow's hierarchy, or the strength of his relationship needs?

This line of motivation theories has been concerned to identify the categories and patterns of human needs. It leads almost inevitably to the conclusion 'everyone is different'. It is true that we can make generalizations which may guide the creation of background motivation systems, but when it comes to the manager dealing with an individual subordinate, Schein's model of 'Complex Man' looks uncomfortably close to the truth:

> 'Human needs fall into many categories and vary according to stage of development and total life situation. These needs and motives will assume varying degrees of importance to each person, creating some sort of hierarchy, but this hierarchy is itself variable from person to person, from situation to situation, and from one time to another.'

In other words, everyone is different and individuals may be different in different situations and will change over time.

The reader may feel that, although 'Complex Man' is a reasonable reflection of reality, it is not too helpful in practice. At least the generalized models of Maslow, Alderfer and Herzberg indicate the sort of organizational and supervisory practices which will allow most people a reasonable degree of job satisfaction and perhaps motivate them to higher performance. But in many situations it is clear

---

A rethink: Sensitivity skills

Arguably the most difficult but also the most rewarding aspects of life for most people involve their relationships with others. People are complicated and dynamic; we surround ourselves with walls – words, images, social mores, status and, paradoxically, silence.

All the theories of human behaviour and human psychology in the world cannot hope to truly reflect our complexity. They can therefore, at best, be of only limited use in helping us to overcome the barriers between each other.

The first step in learning sensitivity is to accept the fact of complexity; the second is to be interested in people enough to want to understand it. The third step is to consider yourself and wonder at your own characteristics. How do others see you? Act, react, experiment, reflect. Take notice of the way others talk to you and respond to you. What does it mean? What has made you the way you are? Where have you been? Where are you now? Where are you going?

Now you can try to find out about others.

Sensitivity to yourself and to others may make you more understanding of their needs and problems. This *may* lead you to be more caring and concerned but this is by no means certain. Learning sensitivity skills is a politically neutral activity; it can lead to awareness of weaknesses as well as strengths; it can be useful in conflict as well as in harmony.

that general statements about motivation are unhelpful. The manager must tailor his actions with much more precision than just working out where people are on Maslow's hierarchy.

The Complex Man model, rather like the more recent theories of leadership, emphasizes the need for managers to learn human relations *skills*, not just simple theories. There are two main prerequisites of human relations skill – sensitivity and adaptability.

Sensitivity involves two levels of awareness: learning about subordinates and their personalities and motivations, and also learning about oneself and how one is perceived by other people.

Adaptability involves learning to use different behaviour patterns in different situations; not just reacting from your basic personality but assessing the situation and acting to affect it in specific ways.

Many training exercises involve self-assessment questionnaires followed by group discussions to compare problems and ideas. Case studies are used to draw attention to specific issues. 'T' groups are a particularly intense form of discussion group in which managers talk about themselves and their work for long periods of time. During this process the personality of each individual is often subject to the closest scrutiny by other group members. It is hoped that in this way it is possible to begin to appreciate the complexity of human nature and to see yourself as others see you – sometimes a traumatic process.

Assessment

The theories of motivation we have analysed so far are known as 'cognitive content' theories. They assume that people have needs for money, belonging,

Figure 16   *Interlinking needs*

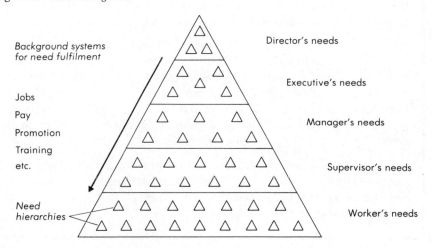

friendship, recognition and so on, to which they react. If the manager can identify the form of these needs and manipulate the means for their achievement, then his purposes can be served as people respond to their internal drives.

Figure 16 provides an organizational overview of this perspective.

The figure shows the implications of cognitive content approaches to motivation if we extend them to all the members of an organization. There is a network of interlinking needs such that at each level the individual is provided with opportunities for need satisfaction by the background systems (pay, promotion, etc.) and by the behaviour of his superior. At the top of the hierarchy the Directors would presumably be motivated to satisfy the 'needs of the organization.'

We have two major criticisms of these theories:

1   The assumption that people are basically passive responders to internal forces is oversimple.
2   The assumption that managers are motivating subordinates towards organizational needs is oversimple.

A rethink: Personal goals

Within the political approach people are seen as active in pursuit of personal goals. They are, of course, constrained in a number of ways. First, their choice of goals may be affected by their socialization (upbringing, schooling, organizational life) and by the immediate pressures on them from family, friends and colleagues. Also they may see that, because of the prevailing political circumstances, only a narrow range of goals can feasibly be pursued. Alternatively, for some, the pursuit of wildly improbable goals may suit their personality. In many situations people may act automatically or emotionally without considering the implications of their behaviour. Goals come to the fore when precedent-setting behaviour is taking place.

Pursuit of personal goals does not mean selfishness or lack of morality. Just because *we* believe our goals are in the wider interest does not make them any less ours. We may feel they are superior on moral, economic, social or any other grounds to the goals of others but *they* may have counter views. In any event the political model relies on no judgement of rights and wrongs. Arguments about the justification of certain goals are of course important aspects of political behaviour.

It is common for people to believe they are not acting 'politically' because what they are doing is 'right' or what they are 'supposed' to do. The party who convinced them of this has had a most powerful political impact on their behaviour.

The political model relies on a picture of man as active rather than reactive, aiming for goals rather than driven by needs. There is a range of theories of motivation which accept this assumption and these are the subject of the next section.

Cognitive process theories

Cognitive process theories of motivation share the basic idea that people take *positive actions* based on thought and decision. They tend to be more concerned with explaining behaviour than seeking ways to manipulate it, and in consequence are often elaborate and complex. We shall outline and discuss a simple version of the best known theory – Expectancy theory, represented in Figure 17. The ideas presented here owe much to Vroom[10] and Lawler.[11]

The diagram shows three basic components of the thought processes underlying behavioural choice:

Figure 17   *Expectancy theory*

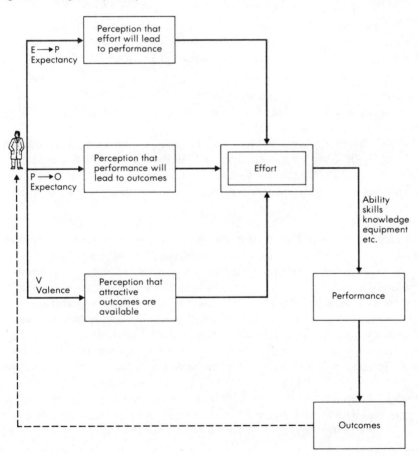

1   E–P Expectancy is the calculation by the individual of whether effort will lead
     to some change in performance.
2   P–O Expectancy is the calculation of whether any change in performance will
     lead to changes in ultimate outcomes.
3   Valence is the weight attached to each potential outcome in terms of its
     desirability.

Effort will be given by the following equation:

$$E = [E - P] \times \Sigma_i \, [(P - 0) \, (V)]$$

(The sigma meaning the cumulative desirability of all the potential outcomes.)
An example should make this clear:

Dave, a junior manager in the Marketing Department is told by his boss, Mary,
that part of his job will now involve using the computer. She tells him that if he
learns well he will be recommended for an upgrading at the end of the year. How
will Mary's statement affect Dave's motivation?

Expectancy theory tells us that Dave's primary considerations will be:

E–P Expectancy: 'Can I learn how to deal with the computer?'
P–O Expectancy: 'If I learn will Mary fulfil her promise of an upgrading?'
Valency: 'How much do I want an upgrading?'

There may be other considerations, of course. Dave may see learning about the
computer as fun, or as having long-term benefits irrespective of any upgrading.
These would add to the list of expectancies and valencies which will fit the
equation and ultimately affect Dave's effort.

Clearly, in order to predict the effect of Mary's statement we would need
to know about Dave's ego (affecting his E–P expectancy), his opinion of
Mary (affecting P–O expectancy) and the relevance of an upgrading to his
personal goals. Hence sensitivity is once again emphasized as an essential
management skill.

There are lessons from the model for Mary. If she boosts Dave's ego and
takes steps to reassure him of both his ability to cope and hers to supply the
upgrading, this may remove obstacles to motivation. She may also be able to affect
Dave's goals by persuasion, education, argument or other interpersonal
techniques.

Figure 17 also shows that effort does not convert directly to performance. If
Dave does not have the required level of ability or is given inadequate facilities and
training, then no amount of effort may compensate. Furthermore, in the longer
term, the consequences of this change and Dave's response will affect future
events. If he learns well and is upgraded, he will have had his belief in himself
reinforced and his faith in Mary justified. He may also develop a higher level of
ambition. Alternatively, if he fails and/or receives no upgrading, then future
changes will be viewed differently. The motivation of an individual is shown
to be a developing process, not to be understood by the study of one-off
events.

Motivation and the political approach

All writers who are concerned with motivation and leadership have developed their ideas in order to help managers understand human behaviour. Most have also suggested ways in which managers can stimulate subordinates towards organizational goals. It is this second focus which gives the subject its managerialist bias, and which we reject as too narrow. We accept the importance of understanding human behaviour and the ways in which it may be influenced; indeed, this is fundamental to the political approach. However, the second focus, instead of simply being concerned with how people can be motivated to work harder, should ask the question 'How can we get people to do what we want?' irrespective of what that is. Furthermore, we do not have to ask this question purely in terms of the manager affecting the behaviour of his subordinates. Any employee can try to get his way and can learn theories and strategies to help him.

Figure 18 shows how blinkered the manager may be if he only studies motivation and leadership instead of the full range of influence possibilities.

The subject of influence will be explored in depth in Chapters 6, 7, 8 and 9. We will show how a rich appreciation of organizational activities and relationships can be based on a study of power. At this stage, however, we shall build the political model of human behaviour which underlies those chapters.

The cognitive process theories of motivation, as we have noted, are closest to the political model. Their fundamental assumption that people are active in the pursuit of goals is the same. Iain Mangham[12] is a writer on organizational politics whose ideas help to clarify the social psychological processes which underpin the radical political view. For him, man is 'sensing, perceiving, interpreting, choosing and adaptive' rather than 'driven by forces within himself or by variables present in the environment' (p. 21). He characterizes man as 'initiator rather than passive reactor' (p. 27).

Figure 18   *The relationship between influence, motivation, and leadership*

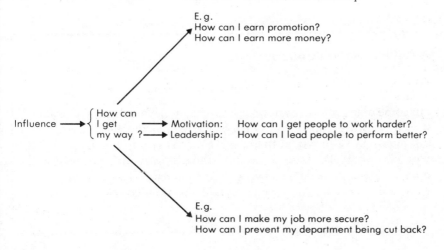

E. g.
How can I earn promotion?
How can I earn more money?

Influence {
How can I get my way ?

→ Motivation: How can I get people to work harder?
→ Leadership: How can I lead people to perform better?

E.g.
How can I make my job more secure?
How can I prevent my department being cut back?

This characterization of man, in turn, opens up the question 'Where do goals come from? In part they are conditioned by the upbringing of the individual, his parents, his schooling, the society in which he lives and so on; in part they reflect his personality and the needs created by his physiological and psychological characteristics; the opportunities and the pressures created by his environment, including his relationships with others, will be important; finally, there is perhaps some element of individuality within us all which may assert itself above all these factors and lead us to pursue goals which could never be predicted from our past behaviour.

A second assumption of the political model is that individuals will formulate *strategies* designed to fulfil their goals, an idea which receives little treatment in the traditional motivation literature. These will be based on an active assessment of the political situation, including such factors as the prevailing circumstances, political capability and potential responses of other parties. As Mangham notes:

'The essence of social behaviour is that the actor is aware of the potential response of others, and selects and shapes his own behaviour accordingly' (p. 47).

The political model emphasizes the necessity for considering relationships between people in order to understand their behaviour. Individuals often combine together into groups, or coalitions, designed to help the members in pursuit of their personal goals. The membership, of an individual, to a number of different coalitions creates both opportunities for political action and pressures, due to the different goals and strategic choices of coalition members.

These three factors – goals, strategies and coalitions – underpin all political models. They are bound together by a fourth factor – power. An individual's perception of his power will affect the goals he sets, the strategies he chooses and the nature of the coalitions he joins.

Motivation research may help to explain how boring jobs, inadequate incentives

---

A rethink: Action and reaction

Man makes the system (action) but the system makes man (reaction).

For some of us, action, as opposed to reaction, is much more possible. If we have power, and if we have learned to question the influences on our minds and behaviour, then we are more likely to see the political model as useful. If, however, we have little power and do not wish to question our conditioning, if we wish to conform and behave as pawns within 'the system', then we may find the political model hard to accept.

or poor working conditions can affect performance, but political research may explain why workers have allowed these conditions to develop without overt resistance and why some managers have been able to impose them against the wishes of both the workers and other managers.

Motivation research may provide some insight into why one group of workers is resisting the introduction of new technology, but the political approach can also suggest *how* the workers might resist, and assess their chances of success.

Andrew Pettigrew studied a group of computer programmers in a particular organization who formed a coalition to defend their status against the new breed of systems analysts.[13] By examining the strategy formulation and strategic processes of the programmers, Pettigrew provides interesting insights into the political nature of human behaviour in organizations.

The programmers, in defending their position against the analysts, tried to use a series of strategies. They claimed the analysts did not have suitable expertise in the handling of computers and could not be considered as their equivalent and certainly not as replacements. They tried to establish myths about the difficulty of their work and its significance to the organization, trying to create the impression that they were indispensable. Also, the programmers kept control of information and tasks by not keeping records or written descriptions. Keeping things in their heads ensured that outsiders could not easily replace them, because work could not be routinized or transferred. Finally, they tried to influence recruitment policies to ensure that programmers retained their importance and high status.

This example demonstrates the inadequacy of abstract theories about the determinants of behaviour, which are divorced from the specific context in which the actors exist and the strategies they may pursue to change things. The theories of Mayo, Maslow, McGregor and Herzberg would not have helped the programmers to resist the threat from the analysts. Nor would they provide much advice to management about how to deal with this situation.

Ian MacMillan has developed a comprehensive and sophisticated political model which extends from the individual in the workplace to the inter-organizational level.[14] He demonstrates the need to be aware that organizations are large coalitions in their own right which are constantly engaged in interactions, often conflicts, with one another.

MacMillan focuses particularly on individual political behaviour and coalition formation, and Figure 19 is a simplified version of his framework.

The starting point is the individual. Let us suppose he has been working for an organization for a few years and has an established position and network of relationships. We start with the basic political assumption that the individual will be 'acting in his own self-interest toward other members or parts of the organisation in the pursuit of his own goals' (MacMillan, p. 50). The individual's goals will relate to his values and interests but will probably also be tempered by his perception of what is achievable. He will have a view of his own political capabilities within the prevailing circumstances. The political actor may be motivated to respond to opportunities and threats which relate to his goals – if he is aware of them and believes they can be affected by his behaviour.

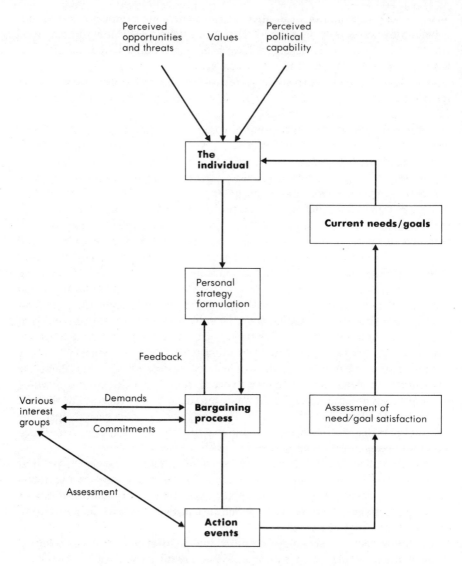

Figure 19   *The political nature of individual action (Adapted from McMillan, 1978)*

In order to achieve his goals, the individual actively formulates a strategy. He is often not capable of doing much on his own, so he will usually seek other members of the firm with whom he can combine for mutual support. This is the process of coalition formation depicted in the centre of Figure 19. It is essentially a bargaining process in which the individual makes certain demands for support and the group demands certain commitments in return. Individuals usually belong to many coalitions which are in a state of flux as demands, commitments and members change.

The process of bargaining with interest groups is rarely overt. Often we do not think of it as bargaining at all. Every employee, for example, is a member of a department which is itself an interest group. He tends to conform to the established patterns, or norms, of behaviour in the department, and in return will be accepted and receive social and perhaps work and career satisfactions. 'Being loyal' to your department, work group or friends, may be something people do in the expectation of some return for being a good member of these interest groups. We work hard at our jobs, perhaps in the expectation that the interest group we are working for (in the widest sense this interest group is the organization itself) will help us achieve our objectives.

Time passes. Things happen. Both our subject individual and the members of the interest groups to which he belongs make an assessment of what is happening. If the individual is unhappy about the return for his efforts he will make new demands, or consider leaving the group, or perhaps reduce his commitment. If strategies are successful and goals are achieved it is likely that our actor will increase his political capability and set his sights on different goals.

We can see that underlying this model is a broader picture of the organization, built on the coalition. As coalitions become larger they cannot meet all the demands of all the members, so they tend to develop a set of 'generalized goals'. The larger the coalition becomes the more generalized become its goals and, usually, the looser the commitment of the members. Large coalitions are usually combinations of smaller coalitions which have come together for specific mutual advantages. It is at this point that we must avoid a trap, that of attributing goals to the organizational coalition which are really those of one powerful interest group within it.

Implications for the practising manager

Before closing our discussion on motivation we shall assess the implications of our analysis for the manager in his daily life. 'Implications' will also be developed from our studies of groups in organizations and organizational culture and climate in the next two chapters. Our aim is to show how the ideas contained in the text should stimulate an assessment process which will lead to more effective behaviour. 'Implications' sections will not be necessary in later chapters because these are directly based on the political model and thus already offer practical insights.

Implications are not the same as prescriptions. All situations are unique, so cut-and-dried solutions cannot be offered. What we will try to do is raise the reader's consciousness of important considerations, improve his ability to comprehend and diagnose, and alert him to possibilities and alternatives.

In terms of motivation, what are the key questions a line manager should ask himself?

What kind of situation am I in?
The nature of the task, the subordinates, the organizational structure, his own personality and position – these are the sorts of factors to be assessed. In particular

he must evalute his subordinates. What are they like? Are they primarily interested in a quiet life? Is their motivation really a problem, or is it their ability or the facilities they have?

Does the task demand great effort, attention to detail, honesty, tolerance of monotony? The manager must be quite clear what he is looking for. This leads in to our next question . . . .

What are my real goals here?

Is the manager concerned about his employees' motivation, or their satisfaction? Does he want to create an atmosphere of friendly co-operation or aggressive competition? Does he want initiative and independence or compliant conformity?

What experience/knowledge do I have to draw on?

Hopefully, the ideas contained in this chapter will help the manager to reassess his experience. Is this a new situation? How does it differ from those he is used to? If it is not new, should the manager act as he has always done? Is this usually effective? Is it time to experiment with slightly, or perhaps even radically, new behaviours?

What alternative do I have?

The manager must be aware of the steps he *can* take to change things. Can he affect salary levels? Can he change the design of jobs? Can he affect promotion decisions? Often there will be considerable constraints on his ability to mediate the things his subordinates desire.

What impact will different actions have?

No one can predict human responses with complete accuracy but the manager must try to evaluate the outcomes of the different actions he may take. He must evaluate *all* the outcomes, not just those which he is aiming for. Will there be side-effects? Might there be after-effects?

The practising manager who reads the above questions may protest that he does not have sufficient time for all this 'thinking it through'. The fact is he cannot afford not to; this may be the most productive way he can spend his time.

The manager who simply reacts on the basis of experience is far less likely to be effective than the manager who has a cognitive map, based on theoretical ideas, which he is continually examining and improving in the light of new experiences. In this chapter we have provided both a conceptual platform and a procedure for tackling reality.

Conclusion

The motivation theory of 'political man' which we have built brings together many aspects of the earlier theories. People in organizations may, in developing their goals, be responding to internal needs or drives. Money can be a major objective, so can security, status and the need to be loved and respected. Power itself can be a goal and for some there is an overwhelming internal desire to be recognized as capable and successful. Friends, family and peers can all apply pressures, often unintentionally, which affect our goals. The important point is that goals are a highly personal matter. In formulating them the individual acts politically, he assesses his situation and, if he is realistic, pursues only those which he may hope to achieve – here his ego is a vital factor, combined with his political awareness and recognition of his own political capability, as well as his personal propensity to take risks.

The process of goal formation cannot be separated from that of strategy formulation. Conventional motivation theories exhort the manager to provide opportunities for the subordinate to achieve his goals (satisfy his needs in fact) whilst at the same time contributing to 'organizational success'. This may be possible sometimes (assuming that organizational success is a meaningful phrase), but many employee goals will not be compatible with such an idea. And, of course, the manager may be more interested in his own success. Thus strategy-making is a much neglected subject in the literature despite its centrality to the lives of all employees. As we showed in Figure 18, simply to focus on motivation strategies is to adopt a partial perspective which is of limited value in practice.

In Chapter 6 we will be examining in much more detail the ways in which individuals possess different power bases which may affect their goals and strategies. In Chapter 7 we will show how important is the context within which organizational behaviour takes place. In Chapters 8 and 9 we will be discussing the strategy-making process.

These four chapters are designed to develop insight into the subject of influence. It is this subject which takes up where motivation leaves off.

References

1   D. McGregor, *The Human Side of Enterprise* (New York: McGraw-Hill 1960)
2   P.F. Drucker, *The Coming Rediscovery of Scientific Management*, Conference Board Record (1976), 13(b), 23–27
    E.A. Locke, 'The ideas of Frederick W. Taylor: an evaluation', *Academy of Management Review*, vol. 7, no. 1 (1982), pp. 14–24
3   E.H. Schein, *Organizational Psychology*, 3rd ed. (Englewood Cliffs, NJ: Prentice-Hall 1980)
4   F.J. Burns Morton, *Foremanship – a Textbook* (Chapman and Hall 1958), p. 281
5   H.G. Hicks and C.R. Gullett, *Management* (New York: McGraw-Hill 1981), p. 482
6   E.A. Fleishman, 'Twenty years of consideration and structure', in E.A. Fleishman and J.G. Hunt (eds), *Current Developments in the Study of Leadership* (Carbondale: Southern Illinois University Press 1973)
    F.E. Fiedler, *A Theory of Leadership Effectiveness* (New York: McGraw-Hill 1967)
    R.R. Blake and J.S. Mouton, *The Managerial Grid* (Houston: Gulf Publishing 1964)

P. Hersey and K.H. Blanchard, *Management of Organizational Behaviour* (Englewood Cliffs NJ: Prentice-Hall 1977)

V. Vroom and P. Yetton *Leadership and Decision Making* (University of Pittsburgh Press 1973)

7   A. Maslow, *Motivation and Personality* (New York: Harper 1954)

8   F. Herzberg, *Work and the Nature of Man* (Cleveland: World Publishing Co. 1966)

and 'One more time: how do you motivate employees?' *Harvard Business Review* (January–February 1968), pp. 53–62

9   C.P. Alderfer, *Existence, Relatedness, and Growth: Human Needs in Organizational Settings* (New York: Free Press 1972)

10   V.H. Vroom, *Work and Motivation* (New York: Wiley 1964)

11   E.E. Lawler, *Motivation in Work Organisations* (Monterey, California: Brooke/Cole 1973)

12   I. Mangham, *The Politics of Organisational Change* (Associated Business Press 1979)

13   A. Pettigrew, *The Politics of Organisational Decision Making* (Tavistock 1973)

14   I. MacMillan, *Strategy Formulation: Political Concepts* (St Paul, Minnesota: West Publishing 1978)

4

GROUP DYNAMICS

Why talk about groups? There are several answers, which we will come to in a moment. We will follow here the format of the previous chapter on motivation by first outlining conventional wisdom on the study of groups. This will involve defining groups, trying to explain how they arise, drawing attention to the many different kinds of groups, and discussing groups in connection with norms, productivity, roles, conflict, and decision-making. Then we will relate this to the political perspective, and conclude with some implications for the practising manager.

Why look at groups?

It is worth looking at the way groups are put together and function for these reasons:

1   Groups tend to develop *norms*, or accepted forms of behaviour, or standards of conduct. These norms may affect the output of work groups, or other ways in which they operate. Again, such norms may affect who can be a member of a group, and on what terms, or they may affect the willingness of groups to initiate or accept change.

2   Sociologists use the term *role* to refer to positions in society associated with particular responsibilities, and from which certain 'performances' are expected. Hence there are citizen roles, various family roles, and occupational roles. With reference to the last, many of these work roles are acted out wholly or partly in groups. So the study of groups may be the real way to find out what it means to be, say, a chargehand in manufacturing, or an R & D project leader in an electronics company, or whatever. Furthermore, within groups individuals may take on some purely group related role, such as counsellor, peacemaker, troubleshooter, or comedian.

3   Groups take *decisions*, or at least are an important part of the context in which decisions are taken. This is at least residually true for blue-collar work groups, and is obviously true for management groups. With regard to the latter,

conventional wisdom is that many management decisions are taken in committees or meetings, so the study of group dynamics becomes the study of the process of decision-making.

Before looking in more detail at these entities – norms, roles, decisions – it is helpful to pose two other questions: what do we mean by groups and how do they arise?

What is a group?

An extensive American-dominated literature on groups has grown up since the end of the Second World War, and this body of writing does offer a fairly consistent idea of what constitutes a group. The definition usually proceeds in terms of three necessary conditions.

1   A group is a collection of people who interact, who have contact, and more than fleeting contact.

2   For it to be a group, these people must be aware of each other – not just nominally or rationally aware of each other's existence, like people sitting in a commuter train who have no intention of ever speaking to each other, but meaningfully or emotionally aware.

3   A group is a group when its members think it is. This third point may seem a bit jaunty, but it is really critical for the development of norms, collective sentiments, and control of behaviour. This idea of some collectivity being confirmed by its own consciousness operates at other levels too. Consider nationalism: as a variation on the theme of group consciousness it is easy to find exceptions to all the arguments about common language, religion or heritage. So nineteenth-century Americans or twentieth-century Swedes have little in common except their conviction about being nations. This awareness or conviction is important for groups, and, while this is recognized in the definitional literature, its implications are sometimes ignored in the discussion.

How do groups arise?

The most simple explanation for the formation of groups is expressed in the single word, propinquity. People who are physically or geographically close tend to satisfy affiliative impulses, the social needs of Mayo and Maslow discussed in Chapter 3, by forming groups. Evidence exists for this view,[1] some of it from residential studies as well as from occupational sociology. The weakness of this propinquity explanation is that it is not very discriminating; sometimes propinquity leads to group formation, sometimes it does not.

A more refined theory of group formation is that of George Homans,[2] based on the idea that activities, sentiments, and interactions directly relate. These three elements, that is, are mutually reinforcing, or increase together. The more activities in which the group engages, the more numerous or frequent or complex will be their interactions; the more they interact or accomplish in common, the more intense will be their sentiments (feelings about each other).

As with propinquity theory, there is nothing absolute about Homans' theory. The three elements, that is, do not necessarily or invariably go together. There are occasions, for instance, when common activities or frequent interactions do not lead to strong sentiments in Homans' sense, or to positive feelings of liking or esteem. Yet Homans has given us a full perspective on group formation, and a dynamic one. In the very substantial book in which Homans develops this theory,[3] he also succeeds in relating it very plausibly to a range of studies of people in contact, including some classic studies of rural communities.

If these theories of group formation are not always compelling, one can get good practical results in terms of them. Or to put it another way, it is often surprisingly easy to get people to form groups in the strong sense we are concerned with in this chapter, perhaps the most famous experimental illustration coming from one of the American boys camp studies.[4]

In this study, two dozen boys, matched in all the relevant ways but who did not previously know each other, were brought together at a summer camp. At first they were allowed to mix freely, making friends and forming relationships at will. But then the organizer-experimenters divided them into two artificial groups which deliberately cut across the previous friendships and patterns of liking. These artificial groups very quickly developed into real and cohesive groups, generating their own leaders, establishing patterns of conduct and sanctions, marking out group territories and assuming groups names (Bull Dogs and Red Devils). At this stage a set of 'who-likes-who' tests showed that the boys' choices were overwhelmingly in-group, although their earlier friends were mostly in the opposite groups.

When the experimenters introduced a series of competitive games, offering pocket knifes as prizes to the overall winners, there was a rapid escalation of conflict between the groups. By the end of the games, in which the Bull Dogs were the winners, the two were engaging in acts of intergroup aggression and retaliation, and hurling at each other not only abuse but also camp crockery!

Military organizations, in particular, obviously exploit and profit from this activity–interaction–sentiments model of group formation, and the ensuing group cohesiveness and *esprit de corps* are often very important for effective combat performance. It is also clear from a variety of war biographies and reminiscences that membership of such groups - bomber crews, patrol groups, tank crews, infantry companies, and so on - is of great psychological moment to those involved, the relevant group, its co-members and identity seeming to transcend previous relationships. The satisfactions obtained in such groups often lead the veteran to mourn their passing despite the dangers and hardships which were collectively and individually suffered.

Types of groups

So far we have spoken of groups as though they were a single phenomenon. But in fact there are some quite important distinctions to make between various types of groups, most of these distinctions appearing in one form or another in the literature.

The first necessary distinction is between formal and informal groups. A formal group is usually defined by conventional writers as one brought into existence by the organization in the pursuit of its objectives. Thus the purchasing section, or the board of directors, or the works council, or the standing salaries review committee are all formal groups. Formal groups may be permanent, as in the case of the examples just given, or only temporary, as in the case of task forces which disband when the objectives set for them are realized (or the time set has passed), and committees set up to handle one-off situations such as a move to a new manufacturing site or a major change in work systems.

Informal groups, however, form in response to human social needs rather than organizational requirements, even if their emergence is shaped or conditioned by the form of the work organization. The groups in the Bank Wiring Observation Room of the Hawthorne Studies described in Chapter 1 are a classic example of informal groups. They satisfy social, affiliative needs of their members rather than company objectives. On the other hand, the emergence of these two groups at the front and back of the Observation Room is contingent on small differences in job content, the front group regarding their work as more difficult and themselves as a little superior. But again these two groups, even if differentiated by job content, actually subvert the company's rules in various ways, by job sharing and job swapping (within the group), for example.

The basic point is that informal groups, as Edgar Schein puts it, 'almost always arise if opportunities exist',[5] pretty well in line with the Homans' theory. Some writers, however, have felt it desirable to distinguish between different kinds of informal groups. A case in point is Melville Dalton in his study of managerial power play in several American companies.[6] Dalton distinguishes firmly between horizontal and vertical groups. A horizontal group is made up of people on roughly the same horizontal level in the same functional area, say a group of salesmen, or field-repair men, or maintenance foremen; whereas a vertical group contains people from different levels. In the production area it might be a foreman–superintendent–production manager group banding together to outwit the quality control department, or put pressure on the maintenance section, or convict the designers on charges of impracticality. One can go further and distinguish mixed or random groups whose members are drawn from both different levels and different functions. These mixed groups, based on an amalgam of personal liking, operational propinquity, and mutual favour rendering, are very common in middle management. Production managers are particularly prone to membership of such mixed groups, thereby enjoying access to information in other departments and the chance to bend the system.

So far we have categorized groups on the basis of whether or not they explicitly serve the organization's goals, in managerialist terms – in other words, the formal versus informal distinction – and in terms of the hierarchical and functional origin of their members – the horizontal, vertical, mixed distinction. Some writers also distinguish between the more formal types of group on a similar basis. Robbins, for example,[7] distinguishes between the command group, the task group and the interest group. The most straightforward of the three is the command group, composed of a boss and his direct or indirect subordinates in formal organizational terms. Thus a project leader, his or her eight researchers, the secretary and three support technicians are a command group; or, in a manufacturing rather than development context, the production manager, his or her production controller, two superintendents, eight foremen and the purchasing manager are a command group.

In contrast, the task group is not so restricted by hierarchy and function, even though it serves some formal organizational purpose. Thus the task group represents those working together to complete some organizational task, and indeed such entities are often called 'task forces' after the military analogy. Higher management might, for example, be concerned about product quality and direct a group of interested parties to work on the question of quality improvement – probably representatives of production, design, engineering, and quality control, chaired by a general manager. Robbins also speaks of the interest group whose members have come together to pursue some objective that concerns them all; unfortunately for our purposes the examples he offers are employee related rather than managerial – defending a colleague faced with dismissal, seeking increased fringe benefits, or changing the holiday schedule.[8]

Finally, there is a different kind of distinction to be made between the membership group and the reference group. All the groups and sub-classifications mentioned so far are membership groups. The membership group is the one to which an individual belongs, whereas the reference group is one with which the individual identifies in some way. Perhaps the individual aspires to belong to the reference group, or feels its standards should be his standards, or the conditions enjoyed by its members should be enjoyed by him, or that the reference group somehow signifies something which he desires or admires.

To give a deliberately loose and non-managerial example, it has been argued by an American historian seeking to explain British economic decline that in nineteenth-century England the landed aristocracy constituted a powerful reference group for rich manufacturers. The latter, that is, sought titles, landed estates, intermarriage with the aristocracy, and public school education and gentlemanly occupations for their sons.

Unfortunately, although the membership group versus reference group distinction is often made, and the concept of the reference group is well established in sociology, little use has been made of it in explanations of managerial behaviour. We will return to the point in the later discussion of group dynamics in the light of the political perspective.

Norms

Much blue-collar and clerical work is done in stable formal groups, with frequent subdivision into informal groups as described in the previous section. Thus the propensity of such groups to develop norms may be critical for their behaviour.

A rethink: Relationships

All relationships between people are political. This is easy to see when we are considering our superiors and subordinates, when we form alliances at work, when we sit on committees, when we negotiate with salesmen, and when we recruit a new typist. But what about our friends, our family, the members of the rugby club and the people we play bridge with at lunchtime?

A relationship is political if power operates between the parties and/or if the parties are relevant to each other's goal fulfilment. Let us examine the first part of this statement. I may have power over my friends, I can persuade them to come for a drink instead of studying, we may exchange favours. Within the family, parents may discipline a child, and yet their desire for the child's love gives the child power too. Even between lovers power is an important variable; one may change normal behaviour patterns in order to please and, of course, there is the more obvious 'If you loved me you would . . .'

What about the second part of our statement? Relevance to goal fulfilment creates *potential power*. Four of us may play bridge every day for a year; it does not *feel* like a political relationship but we provide each other with satisfactions. Suppose one of us decides not to play. Those who remain may be deprived of our game; we have to persuade him to return, offering him a feeling of importance – emotional satisfactions in return for his effort. Perhaps we have to offer (or threaten) more if there are no alternative players.

Politics is a most pervasive phenomenon.

At this point in the exegesis it has become *de rigeur* to cite the informal groups of the Bank Wiring Observation Room in the Hawthorne Studies. These do offer a magnificent illustration of work related norms. The workers concerned had norms which firmly regulated output in that there were norms against rate busting (producing too much) and chiselling (doing too little) and the tactical concealment of completed work was also sanctioned. Furthermore, as mentioned earlier, the members engaged in job sharing and job swapping, although these were not officially allowed, and consistently bailed out one of the inspectors, as well as having an informal norm against acting officious (buddying or overco-operating with foremen).

But norms restricting output or co-operation with supervisory authority are far from being the whole story. Informal norms may also dictate who, in family or even ethnic terms, may become members of certain work groups. Becoming a docker, for example, is not an occupational option open to all comers, but is in practice restricted to the brothers and sons of those who are dockers already. Neither is this mechanism invariably restricted to heavy, traditional blue-collar jobs. The London-based barristers' clerks, for example, who enjoy an enviably high income for organizing and stage-managing the work of the practice, have made these jobs virtually hereditary.

A variation on this theme is that there are some occupations whose numbers are strongly patterned as to personality behaviour, such that informal norms restrict or condition entry in these terms. A study of navvies working on construction sites in the north of Scotland, for instance, showed the strong predominance of swearing, drinking, fighting and gambling such as to exclude from the job those not adept in these pursuits.[9]

Or again, there are occupational studies which show that some work-based groups overspill into leisure activities. The Hull trawlermen described by Jeremy Tuxstall,[10] for example, showed that crew-based groups would also expect to socialize at home (on shore). It should be said straight away that this overspill of work groups into leisure is not invariable. Indeed a study of affluent manual workers at three companies in Luton in the early 1960s[11] showed that there was very little carry-over from the workplace to recreation (and not much take-up of company-organized sports or recreational facilities). In other words, the propensity for work groups to overspill into leisure is best seen as a continuum. We probably do not understand all the factors involved in making it more or less likely, though the physical arduousness or dangerousness of the job seems to be one factor in this overspill, as in the deep sea fishermen example.

In so far as informal groups at work are setting norms about output and working methods, they will tend to be resistant to change, at least to management initiated change. Most straightforwardly, any change likely to break up informal groups at work is likely to be resisted. There is also a broader consideration, which is that these informal norms are often an assertion of employee control in the face of management's demands and expectations: they serve to show that workers themselves control output and methods, and place strict limits on the extent to which they will yield to the firm's formal authority. So the cohesiveness of these blue-collar work groups in the sense of the development and enforcement of norms is all about countervailing power. This comes out very clearly in the case of the Hawthorne Studies. This fact of countervailing power does not necessarily mean group practices hostile to management, though they often are; it is more a question of deciding or exercising control for its own sake – employees saying implicitly 'We'll say when it's quitting time!'. On the specific issue of output, the relationship between group cohesiveness and productivity needs to be illuminated.

Group cohesion and productivity

Some evidence seems to suggest that there is a positive relationship between group cohesion and productivity,[12] that where members of a group are strongly attached to each other and strongly committed to the group objectives, productivity goes up. There are, however, two reasons for suggesting that the phenomenon is more complex.

First, it is likely that (high) productivity is a cause of group cohesiveness as well as a result of it. If a group is cohesive then there is little internal friction of a kind likely to inhibit high output, and the ethos of the group will be generally supportive. If higher productivity results, this attainment may serve to reinforce the group's cohesion and enhance the perceived attractiveness of membership of the group, especially where high productivity is rewarded financially as will frequently be the case. Of course the issue of productivity is just a special case of a more general phenomenon, namely the positive effect of cohesion on the achievement of group objectives. To give a deliberately non-industrial example, a football team is undoubtedly a group, and the more cohesive a group it is the better it is likely to play. And if it wins the Cup Final, this in turn will raise morale, self-esteem, the perceived attractiveness of group membership, and so on. It will, that is, increase group cohesiveness.

Second, there is a further complication in the relationship between cohesion and productivity. This is that the relationship will only be positive if the group goals are the same as the formal company goals (that is, in favour of work output, and productivity). Where there is non-alignment between group objectives and typical organizational objectives, then group cohesiveness is likely to work against productivity. This reverse relationship is commonplace in industrial relations where it is clear that the cohesiveness of work groups deriving from the physical danger of the task, the exclusiveness of the occupation in informal recruitment terms, or even the relative remoteness of the occupational community lead to a resolute espousal of group interests *vis à vis* those of employers: coal miners in Britain are a good example on all counts.

The fact that group cohesiveness may have these negative implications for formal company goals of the profit and productivity type is part of a more general phenomenon. Whenever the objectives of the group run counter to those of the organization's senior office holders, group cohesiveness serves to strengthen the resistance. To broaden the issue with another non-industrial example, it is notable that IRA prisoners in British gaols offer much more and better organized resistance to the prison authorities than the ordinary criminal prisoners.

Groups and roles

A large part of our interest in the connection between groups and roles is that it helps us to understand the nature of managerial work. By roles we mean the behavioural regularities which attach to the performance of people in jobs in companies – jobs such as foreman, buyer, personnel officer, or managing director. And the important point is that many of these roles are acted out wholly or partly in groups. So groups are a strategic site for the study of work roles.

If we want to know what a work role is really like, what it consists of in behaviour and performance terms, we need to view it in the group context. Or, as is the case with many management roles, we need to view it in the context of the several groups in which the manager may appear and perform. This is a way of saying that most jobs in management are highly interactive or, in the words of a popular definition, are all about getting things done through people.

There is another strand to this argument, which is that leadership is inseparable from followership, and most management jobs involve some element of leadership. As the earlier discussion of leadership (Chapter 3) showed, there is no 'good leadership' in any absolute sense. What constitutes effective leadership varies according to several contingencies, of which the most important is the people involved. So more sophisticated theories of leadership make a lot of play with the wishes, disposition, needs, and maturity of potential followers. This is one more argument for the study of work roles in a group context. Or to put it another way, practical studies of leadership are studies of individuals at work in groups.

So far we have argued that most management work is highly interactive, that is, most managers spend most of their time with people – talking, listening, persuading, and influencing. In a very basic sense management work is 'people work'. What is more, much of this people work is in the form of actually taking part in formal meetings and sometimes chairing them. It comes out clearly in surveys of the way in which managers actually spend their time that participating in meetings is an important part of most management jobs.[13]

These meetings and committees in which managers are involved are only intermittent groups, but they are groups none the less, and they satisfy the criteria for groups propounded at the start of this chapter. So when we speak of the study of groups illuminating the nature of management work this includes the idea of the behaviour and performance of managers in meetings. There is a final consideration which applies particularly to groups in the form of committees and other meetings.

Such meetings are obviously purposeful, even though the purpose may vary. Sometimes the formal purpose will be about information exchange, or the control of events, or co-ordination, or devising plans, or generating ideas, or solving problems, or taking decisions, or it may well be a mixture of several of these things. One recent study of the work of general and production managers suggests in fact that many of these meetings are multi-competent and go through a variety of issues, some of which are informational, some decisional, some co-ordinative, and so on.[14] So clearly much of the input in such meetings, in the sense of what people actually do and say, will be explicitly oriented to these tasks of information exchange, decision taking, or whatever. But group dynamics research has added a new dimension to our understanding of the way in which these meeting-groups function.

The essence of this understanding is that the functioning of the committee in a formal task sense is facilitated by maintaining its integrity and cohesion as a group. This end is served in turn by inputs or behaviours of a different kind – reducing tension, building solidarity, emphasizing agreement about fundamentals where this is possible, discharging aggression harmlessly, and seeking to raise the morale and mutual esteem of all participants, and so on.[15] These behaviours may be just as important as those directly and manifestly related to stated tasks. And what is more, in groups which meet regularly, if intermittently, these other behaviours relating to the maintenance of the group may be associated with particular group members in a regular way. In other words, people may take up roles which are not formally specified but which are vital for group functioning. This is recognized in the group dynamics literature in general, but its application to management meetings and committees is often missed.

The academic message is that the analysis of group roles will typically reveal participants whose 'output' is socio-emotional and related to group maintenance rather than explicit task accomplishment. And the practical message is that managers running such committees will also be concerned with group maintenance and will be concerned to acknowledge the support of those participants who contribute to it.

Groups and decision-making

Many decisions in business and industry are taken by committees or in meetings. This gives rise to the simple question: Do groups make good decisions, or would it be better for individuals to make those decisions?

Unfortunately, there is no straight answer, and plausible arguments can be adduced to support both viewpoints. It is quite clear that groups do have some distinct advantages. Several people are likely to generate more ideas (solutions to a problem, decision alternatives) than the individual alone. Not only is this simple consideration more or less true by definition, but there is the further point that more ideas are likely to be produced as a result of interactive stimulation. Individuals, that is, will fashion ideas in a group that they would not manage to bring forth alone. Then there is the fact that the group will have a greater pool of knowledge, substantive and circumstantial, than the putative lone decision-maker, and will similarly dispose of a broader spectrum of experience. To these pluses can be added the fact that group decision-making may permit some distribution of labour, with different members of sub-groups exploring different options or decision factors. And again, the group offers the advantage that members may check each other's interpretations and arguments, hopefully screening out the irrational and ill-founded.

On the other hand, some group decision-making is very unimpressive, and there appears to be a variety of possible explanations, some of them contradictory. In some cases, group members will be so alike in their knowledge bases and experience that the advantages suggested in the previous paragraph may not materialize. On the other hand, groups whose members are very diverse may simply fail to communicate effectively at all, and similarly fail to esteem each other's distinctive competence.

Again, the socio-emotional processes of group maintenance referred to in the last section may come to dominate the actual decision-making task, so that more time and energy is spent defusing tension than deciding what to do. Another dysfunctional possibility is that one or two people who have a particular technical or circumstantial mastery of the issue in hand come to dominate the group with their interpretation and recommendations, thereby negating the potential advantages of a group. Yet the two notorious dangers associated with group decision-making are what are called groupthink and risky-shift.

Groupthink and risky-shift

The Groupthink idea has been developed in particular by Irving Janis[16] and used to analyse several dubious (group) decisions in post-war American foreign policy, including the decision to invade North Korea and allow General MacArthur to advance up to the Yalu River (which brought the Chinese into the Korean War), the decision to mount an anti-Castro invasion at the Bay of Pigs in 1962 (a disastrous failure), and the escalation of the Vietnam War by embarking on heavy bombing of North Vietnam.

The features or manifestations of groupthink are that members tend to rationalize any challenge to the assumptions they have made, and apply pressure to deviants to make them conform to the group line. At the same time, dissenting individuals themselves become unsure of their ground, reluctant to voice a 'minority opinion', and tend to minimize to themselves the importance of their doubts. Then the group takes over, participants who remain silent are deemed to be in support, and rocking the boat is treasonous!

The problem with the groupthink idea is 'knowing when'. Janis's formulation clearly has some verisimilitude, yet groupthink is not inevitable and does not happen all the time.

The phenomenon of risky-shift is a special case of groupthink. The essence of risky-shift is that for decisions involving an element of risk those taken by groups are more risky than those produced by individuals.

As one researcher argues it: 'Caution, which members feel privately, may not be communicated in a group setting, and there emerges the impression that other participants are more daring. Once again we have a group situation in which participation may lead to a levelling rather than a sharpening of the differences among members.[17]

Another writer has argued that there are four possible explanations of the risky-shift phenomenon.[18] The first is based on the idea of familiarity with the risk. At first the risk is frightening, yet talking about it and hearing others speak of it somehow domesticates it and makes it less awesome. The second explanation is to do with leadership. It assumes that those members of the group who are most ready to take risks are those who are the real leaders; hence they achieve a certain dominance in the group's deliberations with the result that their (riskier) ideas are more likely to be accepted.

The third explanation is what is called 'risk-as-value'. It is the idea that (at least moderate) risk is 'a good thing' and caution 'a bad thing'. So that group members who are naturally cautious seek to reaffirm their decision-making virility by accepting the riskier alternatives proposed by others.

The last explanation of risky-shift centres around the idea of diffusion of responsibility. The group decision is in a certain way impersonal; if a risky decision is taken and it backfires, it will be difficult to attribute blame to any individual. The group can afford to be bolder than the single person.

Any reader who feels that the research experiments upon which these notions are based may be somehow unrepresentative, is invited to engage in a small experiment. Take three meetings where real decision issues are discussed and see how often options are canvassed in the discussion which the chairman feels are too risky. The chairman's reaction is a good benchmark because by definition he is plugged into an accountability role which enjoins a modicum of caution.

A rethink: Powerlessness

Most of us have experienced the feelings of frustration which arise in a situation where we would like to take action but believe we are powerless. In practice we are rarely powerless in the true sense.

If our boss is making some change we disapprove of then we could try to mobilize our colleagues against him. We might threaten to resign, or on occasion actually do so. We could take some even more extreme action, run the boss over in the car park, burn down the office, pay an unscrupulous private detective to frame him with some criminal offence and so on. OK, these are far-fetched responses that will only be experienced once in a lifetime. But what about more modest and sometimes more subtle responses? To leak the intended change to colleagues who might have been consulted but were not, to artificially accelerate some undesirable consequences of the change, or to point out some negative implication for the workforce to shop stewards – moves of this kind may frustrate the proposed change or its implementation. The possibilities for influencing others are endless for the actor who is prepared to take enormous effort and risks, and who is not constrained by ethical considerations.

This may be an extreme example but it illustrates a major point. Different people have different perceptions of their own power. If we resign ourselves to the idea that we are powerless, we are likely not to search adequately, for political strategies. If we have inadequate sources of power, how can we create new ones? If we are helpless alone, are there others who may help us?

Powerlessness, even where it exists, need not be a permanent state. We can learn from the experience. What resources do we need to obtain to ensure that we have more influence in the future?

We should add that the foregoing is not a full discussion of the decision process; we have simply raised some major points about groups and decisions. Analysis of decision-making as a political process is given in Chapter 9.

Having looked at some of the main issues in the literature on groups, we would like to turn next to a review of this conspectus in the light of the political perspective.

Group dynamics and the political perspective

In essence the political perspective on group dynamics would raise different questions and prompt different studies. Or to be more critical, from the standpoint of the political perspective, conventional group dynamics is not so much wrong, as of limited application; and in the traditional exposé, which we have sought to mirror earlier in this chapter, the fact of this limited application is obscured by various pieces of (unwitting) sleight of hand.

Consider first that group dynamics is about psychological and sociological theory developed from a range of studies – anthropological, community, laboratory and sometimes work group studies. It is not based on original studies of managerial behaviour or derived therefrom.

Second, the pre-eminent role of the Hawthorne Studies in exposés of group dynamics deserves some critical attention. An initial question concerns the typicality of the groups in the famous and much quoted Bank Wiring Observation Room (BWOR). It is usually assumed that the only distinctive thing about the BWOR is the fact that it was *observed*, that the processes of group formation and their manifestations were recorded and immortalized. But wait a moment: these employees were extracted from their normal work milieu and put in the BWOR where the human and spatial dimensions were such as to facilitate observation. But perhaps these dimensions facilitate group formation too.

Put it another way. The BWOR offers the spectacle of over twenty employees able to form groups. They enjoy, that is, face-to-face contact and their interaction is constant. This constant is not impeded by the physical location of these employees, nor by the nature of the task, nor by the noise level, nor by any aspect of the technology. But how common is it to find work situations in which over twenty employees have the facility of continual interaction?

Workers in factory machine shops do not have it – the machines are too large relative to the humans who work them, and twenty people are typically distributed over too great a physical area. Workers on assembly lines do not have it, for reasons of line tempo and spacing. Workers in chemical plants do not have it, common tasks usually being performed by much smaller work teams. Nor do many workers in what may loosely be called service occupations come together in *constant* groups of twenty plus: railwaymen do not, policemen do not, school teachers do not, and neither do postmen, social workers, or shop assistants.

So the BWOR may be an optical illusion. What it has to teach us concerning the propensity to form groups and their behavioural manifestations may be good and true, but perhaps we are being misled as to the putative universality of such groups. And there is another angle.

The BWOR shows us that workers (somewhere, sometimes) generate norms which affect work output. Fine, that is very useful knowledge – for foremen. But what interest does it have for management generally?

The idea can be restated in a more general form. Group dynamics has implicitly fostered two ideas: that groups universally form, and that they invariably develop norms. We are certainly challenging the second, and have some doubts about the first. On the critical question of norms let us consider for a moment a non-industrial example, and take the staff of a university department. The question, 'On what do they have norms?' we can answer on the basis of professional experience.

There are not any norms relating to the central activity of teaching, beyond a loose consensus that one should do a measurable amount of it. But there are no norms saying you have to like it, or do it eagerly, or experiment with new methods or new courses. The same is true of academic research. Many university teachers engage in it, but there is no group norm obliging one to do so: it is a matter of *personal* choice. And much the same applies to publications: although the official expectation is that university teachers should publish, in practice it tends to follow the famous 80:20 rule – 80 per cent of the publications are produced by 20 per cent of the group. What is more, there is not any consensual norm constraining academics to publish (or at least making those who don't feel bad!). If there are not any norms on the central activities of teaching, research and publication among groups of university teachers, then one may doubt the power and prevalence of norms. Again the suggestion is not that group dynamics principles are wrong, but that they have been overplayed.

But let us go further and inquire about group norms among managers. There is a trap here: the big question is not Do managers as a group have norms? but Do groups of managers have them? Managers as a group, say the British national sample, do have characteristic views and attitudes – on free enterprise, capitalism, trade unions, industrial democracy, proper remuneration, tariff policy, and so on. But this is all about rational attitudes, not group dynamics. If we pose the hard question, 'Do groups of managers, interactive groups in the sense of this chapter, develop and maintain norms?' it is difficult to think of research studies explicitly dedicated to finding this out. One can well imagine that such groups do have norms, but imagination is not evidence.

There is another problem about the relevance of the group idea to managers. This is simply that most managers do not work in *constant* groups. The best study we have of the real work of managers, and one which comprises sub-samples of managers from different roles and functions,[19] suggests that managers are typically involved in a *variety* of groups, committees, meetings and negotiations. Exactly the same message comes from a study of production managers in companies in Britain and West Germany.[20] We also find that all types of managers spend some time alone, working in their own offices, so they, again, depart from the BWOR model of the constant group. In short, most groups in which managers participate are intermittent groups, and most managers participate in several of them. Hence there is a limitation on the extent to which group dynamics applies: it applies to some of them some of the time, not all of them all of the time.

What does the political approach demand of group dynamics?

The most straightforward answer is that we need studies of groups of managers to establish the whether and the what of norms and other group characteristics. There really is a need to know how, say, the top management team, or members of the purchasing department, or the personnel section, or those belonging to a development project, or the salesmen in the eastern region, function as groups. To what extent do they share group consciousness? Do they develop norms and what are they? Are there group roles as opposed to straightforward task roles, and so on?

Second, we need studies which recognize the variety and intermittency of most managerial groupings. The political approach entails a focus on 'forms of association' that are between individual roles and the all-encompassing groups of the BWOR or other quasi-laboratory group kinds. The political approach enjoins this focus because this is the managerial real world; this is how the milieu in which managers perform is structured.

Third, there are gains in political understanding to be made by exploiting the idea of reference groups. At the start of this chapter we distinguished between membership groups and reference groups, where the latter exert an influence on non-members. At the moment we can at least hypothesize the implicit use of reference groups by managers. To take a very general example, when British managers collectively adopt a rather defensive posture, claiming to be underpaid and underappreciated in terms of social esteem, they are implicitly using managers in (other) western industrial countries, all of whom are better paid (except the Swedes) as a reference group. Or to take a more specific case, one of the present writers has summarized recent studies of production managers in Britain [21]; a common theme is a generalized dissatisfaction – with pay, conditions, fringe benefits, and promotion chances; production managers, in giving voice to these sentiments, may well be using (better paid) sales managers as a reference group.

Nor do we want to give the impression that this mechanism only works negatively or for the structuring of grievances. Take production managers again. In fact, they tend to exhibit high morale, notwithstanding the relative grievances to which we have just referred,[22] and cite as reasons for their job satisfaction having a tangible output and a great deal of variety. They are using accountants as an implicit reference group! The general point at issue is that there are gains in political understanding to be made from an explicit and systematic use of the reference group idea.

Fourth, managers have a frequent need to reduce intergroup tension and hostility, especially in the form in interdepartmental hostility. We know both from experience and research studies that there is often conflict between line and staff managers,[23] between the purchasing and engineering functions,[24] and between production managers and just about everyone.[25]

Now, group dynamics researchers have interested themselves in the relations between groups, but primarily to show how rivalry and tension between groups leads to solidarity and cohesiveness within groups. The need is for research which helps practitioners to reduce these hostilities where there is a ritual and stereotypical element in them.

Last in this connection, it would be helpful to have better research-based understanding of the way in which informal systems of communication work. The conventional view is that rumour is 'a bad thing' and that most rumours are wrong. The empirical research has already demonstrated that the reality is much less simple. Hershey's study of rumours in six companies found that nearly half of them were wholly or partly accurate,[26] while a study of two American public sector organizations reported 80 per cent rumour accuracy.[27]

What is more, another study by Keith Davis has shown that informal communication in organizations is not always and everywhere the same.[28] Those who have information to impart (informally) may tell everyone, or only those they trust, or only those they come into contact with on a random probability basis. These three models, which Davis calls gossip, cluster, and probability, all involve the informer talking to several others directly, but this study has also identified the possibility of single-strand communications where A tells B, and B tells C, and so on. Now the only study that brings together the two ideas of informal groups and informal communication is Dalton's study of American managers, mentioned earlier,[29] the simple idea being that those who form the group pool the information. The next need is for study of informal information exchange between groups for tactical or whatever other purposes.

Groups, meetings and decisions

In our view there is a bit of sleight of hand in the way in which the conventional group dynamics exposé equates groups with decision-taking in management meetings. The syllogism goes something like this:

> groups have face-to-face interaction
> and they take decisions
> people at meetings have face-to-face interaction
> they are groups too
> they take decisions as well

This formulation is far from being preposterous, and meetings do indeed take decisions (some of them, some of the time). The objection is that the formulation suggests that meetings = groups = decision-taking, in a universal way.

Against this universal formula there are three arguments. Two of them have already been canvassed – that meetings are only intermittent groups, and that meetings do other things besides taking decisions, such as exchange information or facilitate monitoring or control. The third objection is to the implicit assumption that all come equally to the decision-taking. Meetings are chaired, and in industry they are invariably chaired by the person with the highest rank among those present. So, in practice, 'decision-making' may mean the chairman using his rank and influence to get the meeting to accept the decision alternative he or she wants. And even where the chairman does not have a pre-decision in mind, and really wants the meeting to throw up ideas and alternatives, it is likely that this chairman will rapidly identify some alternatives as more pleasing and acceptable than some others.

There are clearly two sides to this, but the side of the rank-and-file member seeking to resist the will of the chairman is probably better understood. The chairman's initiative (and preferred decision) can be frustrated by raising bogus objections, calling for unobtainable information, pointing out to others present how their interests will suffer, playing off sectional interests against each other, appealing to popular prejudice, and, if all else fails, common-sense objections can be put. What is less well understood is what the chairman may do to get his own way, and this is what managers need to know.

Groups and influence

In viewing conventional group dynamics wisdom in the light of the political perspective we have made several criticisms: that the group dynamics lobby has overplayed its hand in assuming managers to be like workers and workers generally to be like BWOR workers; that meetings have been too facilely equated with groups; and even some of the formal power variables have been ignored.

Yet with all this it remains true that much of the time managers who are trying to get things done, or get their own way, are doing this by influencing groups, albeit transient groups, rather than individuals. Change, in particular, is resisted by groups and can only be engineered by working on groups. These basic considerations make imperative the need for some new focus in group research.

Implications for the practising manager

The ideas on group dynamics have considerable diagnostic value which can be well expressed in terms of critical questions.

What kind of situation am I in?
Do the people whose co-operation I seek form a group? If so, what are its norms and the objectives we all subscribe to? Does it have norms/goals imposed on it from outside?

Does the change I wish to effect involve acceptance by a group: if so, what is the group's likely posture?

Does my initiative involve responses from several groups? If so, will they respond differently, can they be reconciled, or can the disagreement be used tactically?

What are my real goals here?

Do I want to be in this informal group: will it help me to do my job better, get things done easier, or just alienate others who are not in the group either?

Do I want to change group norms (say to get higher output, or acceptance of change) or just sabre-rattle?

Do I want them to find an answer, or accept mine?

What experience/knowledge do I have to draw on?

Do I know what the informal groups are: who is in them, what ties them together (is it all R & D people, a committee to knife the managing director, or just all Glaswegians stick together?) and what are they after?

The last time I went against group norms, did I get anywhere? The last time the group tried to get me to change, did they get anywhere? Will it be different now I am boss?

What alternatives do I have?

For any group of which I am an active or potential member, what are my options: join or not join, stay or leave, conform or not conform, submit, subvert or inspire?

Can I choose to support or not support the person directing this meeting? If I support, can I:

'take out' fractious opposition?
defeat opposition by playing group against group? or by appealing to common interest?
take on a group maintenance role?

Can they choose to support or not support me in my running of this committee or meeting?

Are other groups available which we can take as reference groups?

What impact will different actions have?

If my subordinates form a group, or if I facilitate group formation, will they perform better? or just be better placed to put me down?

In this new situation (new site, new project, new task force) what groups are likely to emerge, with what norms and practices?

How will this takeover/major change/new boss affect existing group loyalties and informal systems?

References

1   Leon Festinger *et al.*, *Social Pressures in Informal Groups: A Study of Human Factors in Housing* (Stanford University Press 1963)
2   George C. Homans, *The Human Group* (New York: Harcourt Brace & World 1950)

3   *ibid.*
4   M. Sherif and C.W. Sherif, *An Outline of Social Psychology* (New York: Harper & Row 1956)
5   Edgar H. Schein, *Organisational Psychology* (Englewood Cliffs, NJ: Prentice-Hall 1965)
6   M. Dalton, *Men Who Manage* (New York: Wiley 1959)
7   Stephen P. Robbins, *Organisational Behaviour: Concepts and Controversies* (Englewood Cliffs, NJ: Prentice-Hall 1979)
8   *ibid.*
9   A.J.M. Sykes, 'Navvies: the work attitudes', *Sociology*, vol. I (January 1969)
    A.J.M. Sykes, 'Navvies: the social relations', *Sociology*, vol. I (April 1969)
10 J. Tunstall, *The Fishermen* (McGibbon Kee 1962)
11 J.H. Goldthorpe *et al*, *The Affluent Worker in the Class Structure* (Cambridge University Press 1969)
12 L. Berkowitz, 'Group standards, cohesiveness and productivity', *Human Relations*, vol. 7 (1954), pp. 509–19
13 Joanna Buckingham and Peter Lawrence, 'The real work of managers', in P.A. Lawrence and C.K. Elliott (eds), *Introducing Management* (Penguin 1985)
14 Peter Lawrence *Management in Action* (Routledge and Kegan Paul 1984)
15 Robert F. Bales, *Interaction Process Analysis* (Reading, Mass.: Addison Wesley 1950)
16 Irving L. Janis, *Victims of Groupthink* (Boston: Haughton Miffin 1972)
17 J.P. Campbell *et al*, *Managerial Behaviour, Performance and Effectiveness* (New York: McGraw-Hill 1970)
18 Russell D. Clark. 'Group-induced shift toward risk: a critical appraisal', *Psychological Bulletin* vol. 76, no. 4 (1971), pp. 251–70
19 Rosemary Stewart, *Contrasts in Management* (McGraw-Hill 1976)
20 Lawrence, *Management in Action*
21 Peter Lawrence, 'Operations Management: Research and Priorities', Report to the Social Science Research Council (London 1983)
22 *ibid.*
23 Dalton, *Men Who Manage*
24 G. Strauss, 'Tactics of lateral relationship: the purchasing agent', *Administrative Science Quarterly*, vol. 7 (September 1962)
25 K.G. Lockyer and S. Jones, 'The function factor', *Management Today*, (September 1980), pp. 56–64
26 Robert Hershey, 'The grapevine – here to stay but not beyond control', *Personnel* (January–February 1966), p. 64
27 Eugene Walton, 'How efficient is the grapevine', *Personnel*, vol. 28, (1961), pp. 45–49
28 Keith Davis, 'Management communication and the grapevine', *Harvard Business Review* (September–October 1953), p. 45
29 Dalton, *Men Who Manage*

5

ORGANIZATION CULTURE, STRUCTURE AND CLIMATE

The aim in this chapter is to deal with the three related, and complicated, phenomena of culture, structure and climate. Some aspects of structure have been discussed already in Chapter 2 in the context of contingency theory, but the idea of culture, and its variant climate, are new. We will start with culture.

Culture

Culture has something in common with atoms: you can see where they have been but you can't actually see *them*. Or more properly, there is something both intangible and ineluctable about culture. We can define it, suggest methods for determining what it is in particular cases, say why it matters, say why it is important, make analytical distinctions about its nature, even explain why the concept of corporate culture is in vogue in the late 1980s. What we cannot do is give a comprehensive or generally agreed account of the various dimensions in terms of which corporate culture can be mapped from organization to organization.

What is corporate culture?
The basic idea of culture, including corporate culture, is that it consists of shared meanings and common understanding, and that this culture is variable from company to company. These views are strongly espoused by Handy, for example, who argues:

> 'For organisations are as different and varied as the nations and societies of the world. They have differing cultures – sets of values and norms and beliefs – reflected in different structures and systems. And the cultures are affected by the events of the past and by the climate of the present, by the technology of the type of work, by their aims and the kind of people that work in them.'[1]

Handy's definition is both representative and interesting. It defines culture conventionally in terms of norms, values and beliefs, asserts that organizational or corporate culture is infinitely variable, and suggests a multiple aetiology – a set of causes from past to present, people to technology. It is worth pointing out right away that the relationship between culture and structure is particularly complicated. In the short passage just quoted Handy claims that structure and systems are a manifestation of (differing) culture. On the other hand, structure is sometimes treated as (part of) a determining framework for organizational culture – as, for instance, when one argues that the premium placed on, say, managerial initiative and freedom, a part of the culture of some company, is facilitated by the high level of decentralization, with decentralization being a structural variable.

It may be that this 'shared meanings' concept of corporate culture is a little too passive. It says more about the 'how' than the 'why' of culture. Another contribution to the debate about corporate culture, that of Edgar Schein, takes a more dynamic view in positing why an organizational culture necessarily develops:

> 'Organisational culture is the pattern of basic assumptions that a given group
> has invented, discovered or developed in learning to cope with its problems
> of external adaptation and internal integration, and that have worked well
> enough to be considered valid and, therefore, to be taught to new members
> as the correct way to perceive, think and feel in relation to those problems.[2]

This definition is a dynamic advance. It tells us why, and in response to what, the culture has developed, and introduces a further new element – that of the teachability or transmittability of culture. If the culture has come into being for powerful reasons, and works 'well' enough, it will be transmitted to new organizational members. It will be the culture in which they are socialized.

How did it start?
It is worth pausing for a moment to ask how the idea of corporate culture started. The straight answer is that the basic idea of culture has been adopted from anthropologists and sociologists and used in a delimited way to add a new dimension to our understanding of how organizations work. This is not to say that anthropologists and sociologists have produced a unified and unvarying view of culture: there is indeed a famous source which reviews no less than 164 definitions of culture.[3] The twin ideas of shared meanings and adaptive response, mirrored in the two definitions quoted above, are however basic to many of these definitions.

Although the notion of organizational culture is at present rather in vogue, it is in fact some time since the concept of culture and the study of organizations were brought together. This was done originally by the American sociologist Philip Selznick, best known for his study of the Tennessee Valley Authority (TVA), an organization set up by Roosevelt in the early 1930s. Its tasks were to administer the damming of the Tennessee River, production of hydro-electric power in the region, and the stage management of its industrialization.[4] Part of Selznick's theory is that the early TVA leaders fostered what was called 'the grass roots ideology', the notion that TVA derived a mandate and authority from the ordinary Americans in the largely poor and rural south east States who were (to be) TVA's

A rethink: The tangibility of culture

A simple exchange

Sociology student   I would like to ask you about this organization's corporate culture.

General manager   We don't waste our time on air-fairy twaddle like that. We're here to make fork-lift trucks.

Sociology student   Thank you for straightening me out right at the start. Don't you mean make and *sell* fork-lift trucks?

General manager   Sorry, when you make them as well as we do, they sell themselves.

Sociology student   Is that what your salesmen think?

General manager   They're not paid to think, they're too busy seeing our customers, finding out how many more they want.

Sociology student   So this is a production led company, right?

General manager   Design and production. Got to design them right as well as make them good.

Sociology student   I suppose that means you take on lots of young science graduates with plenty of good design ideas?

General manager   . . . You what! Practical design is what we're good at. You want to be design director here, you start as a tool room apprentice.

Sociology student   Does your managing director approve of this view?

General manager   Approve of it! He is it! Started on the shop floor at fifteen. Most of the board are ex-apprentices. No college boys here, we're all grafters.

Sociology student   What's company policy on co-determination? Do you have a works committee?

General manager   None of that. When we've got something to tell them, the Old Man lays it on the line for them. When they've got something to tell us, well, we usually pick it up Friday night at ten pin bowling.

Sociology student   It doesn't sound as if you stand on ceremony here.

General manager   You kidding. Know where the directors went for their Christmas lunch last year? Joe's Hamburger Saloon. Old Man's always liked a good hamburger since that sales trip to Minneapolis years back.

Sociology student   Well I mustn't take up too much of your time.

General manager   Don't worry. It is just that I don't know anything about whatever you said at the beginning.

beneficiaries. Again this idea of the special mandate was very convenient in legitimating an unusual organization, created by Roosevelt by administrative fiat, whose operations spanned several States, but which was not a Federal agency in the normal sense. Such an administrative anomaly needed a new support ideology, and the grass roots ideology was particularly good for making TVA independent of existing State and Federal authorities.

In a later book Selznick expanded and generalized this thesis.[5] His argument is that organizations have values (the substance of corporate cultures) and that the role of organization leaders is to fashion, represent and sustain these values. In other words, leader = corporate culture creator.

Why is corporate culture in vogue?

Two different forces, middle-term and short-term, have come together to fashion and foster the current interest in corporate culture. Let us begin with the middle-term development. The 1970s saw a rising interest in international comparison in the social sciences generally, and a particular interest in economic and managerial comparisons. This period has given us comparative studies of management qualifications[6]; studies of the structure of companies in France and West Germany[7] as well as in Britain[8]; research on the development of divisionalization in business firms in France and Germany[9]; comparisons of productivity between Britain and West Germany[10]; studies of work attitudes of multinational employees in several countries[11]; and on occasion characterizations of management in other countries, for example, West Germany[12] and Sweden,[13] as well as EEC related comparative studies, for instance on competitive policy.[14]

In Britain these primarily inter-European comparisons coincided with public awareness of relative British economic failure, or at least underperformance. So that in Britain there has been a practical interest in some of these comparisons: do other countries 'do it better', how do they do so, are they different, and are these differences interesting and relevant to economic performance?

At the same time it would be a mistake to assume that these studies deal only in hard facts – in GNPs and productivity data – in proportions of graduates and numbers of divisionalized companies, for instance. In fact many of these studies embrace a discussion of cultural variables – of attitudes, and values, and dispositions, and states of mind – or serve to highlight differences in the national culture context. To give just one example, the Finniston report on engineering education did not deal only with courses, syllabi and the employment structure, but included discussion of such cultural phenomena as attitudes to engineering in France and Germany, the concept of *Technik* (the knowledge and skills relevant to manufacture), and the role of engineering in German society. And this is a report of a Royal Commission, processed by civil servants!

The shorter-term consideration in the development of interest in corporate culture is more about the American response to the Japanese. In the early 1980s both Europe and America have been dazzled by the economic power and performance of Japan, and this has given rise to a substantial literature seeking to identify the distinctive character and strengths of Japanese management.

This literature as a whole has drawn attention to the differing cultural context of Japan, and to culture-embedded differences of management style. This message has been sharpened by three further influential American books, all from the early 1980s, whose authors were all in contact and engaged in the joint development of ideas. Two of these books, by Athos and Pascale,[15] and Ouchi,[16] respectively, examine Japanese management with particular reference to culture and style, and argue the case for analogous developments in American corporate culture and management style. The third of these books, by two McKinsey executives, Peters and Waterman,[17] is about top performing American companies and what makes them tick. The fascinating thing is that their account is very much in terms of culture and values rather than in terms of management systems or organizational structures. The message seems to be that the success of these top firms in the USA is to a large extent the result of their approach to people, the emphasis they place on communication with customers, their entrepreneurial values and their penchant for action.

In short an amalgam of comparative studies, involving both analysis of Japanese management and its implications for American companies, and an interpretation of the strengths of top US firms, has brought about the firm realization that corporate culture may have a major impact on organizational activity and performance.

Is corporate culture important?

The most general answer to this question is that the idea of corporate culture helps us to describe and understand organizations better. We can only answer fully the question, What is such and such a company like? by making some reference to its corporate culture. But this is not all.

A strong and functional corporate culture will be a powerful cohesive force and facilitate concerted action in particular directions. Now the use of the word functional in this sentence begs the issue a little bit, but it is possible to offer a general definition and examples. A business firm needs to do certain things, firstly, to survive and, secondly, to be a success in conventional business terms. And there will be some variation in what these 'certain things' are, at least in terms of relative emphasis, from case to case, from time to time, and in changing environments. In so far as the corporate culture of a company is in line with these needs, it is functional, and if it is strong as well as functional it will make the success of the company much more likely. In managerialist terms, when we speak of the corporate culture being in line with needs, we mean does it emphasize the right things, does it include appropriate dispositions, does it put a high value on managerial qualities, operating styles, and means of achievement appropriate to its success?

Let us take an example. Suppose a company faces a need to raise the quality of its product and that this is essential for survival. Perhaps its corporate culture, Peters and Waterman style, values highly direct contact with customers. If so, that would be helpful in meeting the new quality demands: the company through key managers would have more feel for the precise nature of customer-desired quality improvements. Or again, perhaps the corporate culture contains a strong element of pride in being a technological leader, in being an early adopter of technical or manufacturing innovations. If so, that could well be helpful in achieving the new quality goals through the selective introduction of robots or installation of flexible manufacturing systems. Or perhaps the philosophy and practice of employee participation is part of the culture; this again would be helpful in engaging the will and interest of workers in achieving higher quality, benefiting from their suggestions on work methods or their enthusiastic participation in quality circles. What is more, if the culture is generally favourable to change, that will be an immense help in adopting measures to raise quality.

It should be added that none of the particular things mentioned in the example in the last paragraph can be taken for granted. Indeed it would be very easy to find examples of companies faced with the same need to raise quality which are in fact traditionalist, change-resistant, technical Luddites who believe that customers can be shut up with another dose of promotional advertising while the same old junk is unloaded on the market.

To go back to the level of the general again, corporate culture is important because it sets limits on what companies can and cannot do (at least without changing the culture, which is slow and difficult). So the nature of the culture will be important, perhaps decisive, for the company's ability to respond to particular challenges, adapt to outside demands and pressures, overcome difficulties, survive mergers or takeovers, diversify, make a success of acquisitions, and implement strategic policy changes. This is a good deal.

What does corporate culture do?

In responding to this question we can give more substance to the ideas canvassed in the last section. Probably the most systematic formulation on the ends served by a company's culture is that of Edgar Schein whose definition of culture was quoted in the first section.[18]

We have already introduced Schein's idea that business organizations face two sets of demands: for external adaptation and survival, and for internal integration. Let us take first external adaptation.

Schein sees five elements to the adaptation and survival imperative, and these are the questions of strategy, goals, means, performance measures and correction systems. Strategy means developing agreement on what the company's main task is; goals refer to agreement on tangible objectives; means is about agreement on the ways (organizational structure, system of rewards) by which these objectives are to be accomplished; performance measures concern agreement on criteria for determining how well the company is doing in the pursuit of these goals; and correction is about agreement on what to do if the company appears to be failing.

There is a corresponding set of imperatives on the internal integration side, which largely parallel the conditions of group cohesion explored in the last chapter. They are almost 'common language', in the metaphorical sense of shared meanings and ease of communication, about organizational boundaries and criteria for membership, and about legitimations of the way power, status and rewards are distributed.[19]

Two further thoughts on Schein's formulation are in order. First, we have pursued it precisely because it is a strong, rather than a representative, conceptualization of culture. In other words, it is valuable because it shows how far the idea can be taken, how all-embracing it can be made. Second, it provides an analytic vocabulary for dealing with particular cases of consequences of corporate culture for performance. If we wish, for example, to identify the culture of company X and then go on to ask how suited this culture is to some new challenge faced by the company – we can do this in terms of strategy, goals, means, and so on.

How can corporate culture be diagnosed?

It should be said straight away that this is not a cut-and-dried exercise like counting the number of widgets in the company store. Several writers have, however, squared up to this problem.

One of these is Vijay Sathe who belongs to the main line 'shared meanings' view of culture[20]. Sathe's argument is that even if these shared understandings, as he calls them, cannot be directly appraised, they will be manifest in four other classes of entity – shared things, shared sayings, shared doings, and shared feelings. To give one of Sathe's numerous examples, a company might be committed to the view that operating informally is desirable. This would be a shared understanding, or one dimension in the corporate culture. This in turn might be manifest in terms of various doings and sayings such as managers working in their shirt sleeves, the absence of reserved parking lots for senior people, maintaining close relationships with the trade union, and in sayings of the 'We don't stand on rank here' kind.

Another writer, Alan Wilkins, has propounded the idea of 'the culture audit'[21]. He argues that the most powerful aspect of culture is shared and taken-for-granted assumptions, such as might be inferred from popular stories exchanged by managers, the routine behaviour of employees, the kind of language used by organizational members, and so on. Now since any comprehensive analysis of the totality of these assumptions would be a big job, Wilkins recommends concentrating on two key areas. These are what he calls implied work assumptions, including assumptions about means and ends, and implied reward assumptions, including the way individual interests are served, and questions of equitable treatment. Deciding on the basis of statement or behaviour what assumptions are implied in these two critical areas is the cultural audit. What is more, Wilkins argues that it will have a diagnostic value for managers or supervisors: they will identify assumptions, assess whether they are functional, and have a starting point for the initiation of any desirable change.

Or again, Edgar Schein has suggested four approaches to the identification of corporate culture, these four being used in combination.[22]

First is the analysis of what Schein calls the process and content of socialization. In practice this means interviews with 'socialization agents' such as foremen, or old and respected members of peer groups, to discover what it is that they think worth passing on to new employees as team members and how they aim to do it.

The second approach is to analyse responses to critical incidents in the organization's past. The interest here is to see what was done in these crises, what was the organization's response in these critical incidents, and why. From the actions and reasons one may reasonably infer elements in the corporate culture.

Schein's next idea is that there is clearly some mileage in analysing the values, beliefs and assumptions of 'culture carriers' or 'culture creators'. This means, in practice, interviewing founders, or current leaders, or other influential members; the aim is to establish their objectives, their way of going about things and their assessment of outcomes. In conducting such interviews, Schein's two itemizations of what constitutes external adaptation and internal integration, discussed in the previous section, may be used as checklists.

The last idea is that the investigator may explore and analyse any anomalies or puzzling features which have emerged in interviews or in the process of observation, and do this with insiders. The key consideration is that the incident must be puzzling, or appear anomalous, to the observer–outsider. If it puzzles him, then it cannot be explained in terms of conventional wisdom, or manifest rationality, or the observer's basic assumptions. So having it explained is bound to

---

A review: Information

Information and the related attributes, expertise, skill, ability and understanding, can give power. It facilitates skilled political strategy formulation; it can lead to better, quicker actions. It can encourage others to follow you. It can make you important for the services you provide, perhaps even indispensable.

This helps to explain the current phenomenon of the 'information revolution'. There is a massive development taking place in the study of management decision-making techniques. This accompanies the explosion in our ability to collect and analyse data using computers.

Information in itself does not give power. It is the analysis of that information, its timeliness, its relevance and its use which count. A common situation these days is one of information overload. What should we leave out? What should we aggregate? What should we analyse statistically? Those who make such decisions can have a strong influence over the impact of the data. Providers and analysers of information are often politically powerful.

All decision-making techniques are attempts to choose between alternatives in the light of particular goals. Much may be delegated to machines, but goal setting must be retained as an inevitably political human activity.

illuminate some assumption or shared understanding peculiar to organization members.

Probably none of the approaches canvassed in this section are watertight, or likely to yield perfect results. But there is some mileage in all of them, and they do serve to show that reasonable attempts can be made to understand the intangible phenomenon of corporate culture.

Of what does corporate culture consist?

This is the most difficult question posed so far in this chapter, not in the sense that it cannot be answered but in the sense that it cannot be answered comprehensively. The identification of *recurrent* elements in corporate culture proceeds by common sense, experience, and inspiration, and it is difficult to put limits on any of these, especially the last.

To unpack this last sentence a little it may be helfpul to offer some illustrations. First, someone will say that whether or not a company is decentralized will be *a* determinant of its corporate culture, indeed a significant element in that culture. This is a common-sense proposition, it is true, and it is easy to illustrate. Second, someone else, on the basis of their experience in, say, a military unit, will say that rule-breaking on a massive scale is permitted in combat situations, but not in peacetime. This is not common sense, it is not obvious (until you have experienced it), but it is true. Third, someone else, say Peters and Waterman, will come along and say, on the basis of their examination of top American companies, that constant and meaningful dialogue with customers is an important dimension of corporate culture, and one which is critical for human success.

These examples show the problems of attempting a comprehensive coverage. We have no way of knowing even when we have codified (all of) common sense; our understanding of the world will never catch up with our experience of it, and inspiration is by definition unprogrammable. With these 'heavy duty' qualifications Figure 20 depicts some of the variable limensions in terms of which the culture of particular companies may be plotted.

Two points should be made about Figure 20. The first is that it is meant to be helpful, to map a little bit of 'the known world', but that is all it does: it is not a comprehensive enumeration, for the reasons given earlier. The second is that in seeking to give some substance to the concept of corporate culture we have introduced some structural variables – tightly or loosely structured organizations, division of labour, degree of hierarchy, and so on. This leads to a new variable and a complex relationship.

Structure

The focus in this section is not to embark on a painstaking review of the whole literature on structure, but to indicate briefly the main line of development, and then to consider the relationship between structure and culture.

The idea of structure 'started off simple'. It figures pre-eminently in the

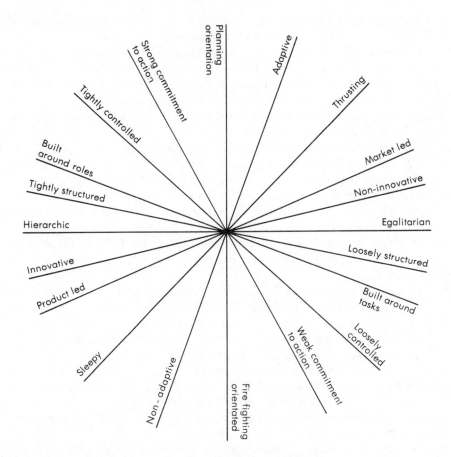

Figure 20   *Variable dimensions of culture in different organizations*

classical management writings alluded to in Chapter 1. In this phase, structure means more formal and tangible things – the organizational hierarchy, the chain of command, the division of labour, the delimitation of functional responsibilities, the designation of who reports to whom, and so on. Or to put it simply, in 'the good old days' structure was about what was on the organization chart.

This has changed, in that structure is now analysed and conceptualized in terms of at least semi-abstract phenomena. Lawrence and Lorsch, for example, have built a theory around the complex relationship between environment-adaptation, differentiation, integration, and performance (see Chapter 2).

In the later, more sophisticated literature, there is one major theme, and two variations. The theme, in a word, is covariance. It is about the variable relationship between structure and other phenomena, about how structure varies dynamically in association with non-structural phenomenon.

The first variation is about the relationship between the organization and its environment. The basic idea is that different environments will give rise to differently structured organizations. Or to put it dynamically, a change in a given environment will, may, or should inspire a change in the organization.

The main American contribution to this structure–environment theme is the work of Lawrence and Lorsch,[23] discussed in Chapter 2 and referred to briefly above. The essence of their theory is that increasing challenge from the environment will lead to an increasingly differentiated company structure in the sense of more discrete and specialized functions within the company. This in turn creates an internal company need for integration, the bringing together of these discrete functions, and the bridging of the organizational gaps. And the final part of the story is that company success or performance is determined by how well this need for integration is met.

The corresponding British contribution to this debate is the work of Burns and Stalker.[24] Their starting point is again the challenge from the environment in terms of the availability of new technology or the need to adapt to new markets. These phenomena are studied by Burns and Stalker primarily by focusing on various Scottish and then English companies in, or entering, the electronics industry in the 1950s.

The concern of Burns and Stalker is not with differentiation and integration, but with the existence, or emergence, of two broad structures, which they call mechanistic and organic. The mechanistic structure is a rather bureaucratic one, marked by high division of labour, discrete tasks, and primarily vertical channels of communication. The organic structure, on the other hand, stresses the possession of relevant knowledge and experience rather than formal authority, and is much looser, with horizontal and criss-cross contact and communication.[25] The simple message is that the mechanistic structure is appropriate for organizations in a stable environment but that an organic structure is desirable for companies adapting to technological or market change.

The second variation on the theme of covariance is the interest in the relationship between the organization's formal objectives or goals, the structure, and the technology employed. Again, the classic work in this tradition, that of Joan Woodward, has already been propounded in Chapter 2. Her basic thesis is that different technology types or production systems – unit, mass, or process – are associated with broadly different organizational structures.

What is more, the Woodward thesis rather more subtly makes connections between goals and structure as well. Although all these companies may be presumed to aim at profitable output and satisfied customers, Woodward is suggesting that they will emphasize different things – design capability, cost-effective production, marketing virtuosity – to attain these ends. And the things so emphasized will be reflected in the structure.

Structure and culture

Our particular interest in this chapter is in the coming together of structure and culture. It was suggested in the discussion of the variable dimensions of culture depicted in Figure 20, that there is a twofold relationship between structure and culture. The first possibility is that one views structure as a part determinant of culture; one argues, for instance, that the corporate culture of a highly centralized, tightly controlled company will be different from that of a decentralized autonomous one. The second possibility is that structural items are actually viewed as part of the culture; where one argues, for instance, that a short chain of command or absence of graded ranks is part of the company's egalitarian culture.

There does not seem to us to be a right or wrong answer. Both interpretations are viable, and it is useful to point to the fact that both exist, and are analytically distinct.

Culture, structure and compliance

One theorist who has operated very much on this boundary between culture and structure is the American sociologist Amitai Etzioni. He takes the compliance structure as the independent variable in his major work.[26] The compliance structure represents those power resources and actions which ensure that rank-and-file participants in the organization do what the dominant élite wants. Maybe they are threatened with violence or restriction of personal liberty, maybe they are exposed to financial rewards and sanctions, or maybe they are manipulated by an appeal to their values and convictions. These three options are denoted respectively as coercive, utilitarian, and normative compliance structures. This is the first building block.

The second is Etzioni's view that organizations may be classified according to the nature of their formal goals. So there are organizations with order goals, such as prisons and detention centres and many mental hospitals; others with economic goals, most obviously industrial and commercial organizations; and organizations with what Etzioni calls culture goals, such as churches, religious foundations, the more ideological political parties and educational organizations. (His system allows for dual purpose organizations and hybrids.)

Etzioni then brings these two ideas together suggesting a natural congruence between the type of goal and the usual compliance system, as indicated in Figure 21

Figure 21 *Relationship between type of goal and compliance system*

		Type of goal		
		Order	Economic	Culture
Type of	Coercive	X		
compliance	Utilitarian		X	
structure	Normative			X

by the crosses. That is to say, organizations with order goals typically adopt a coercive compliance structure, and so on.

Etzioni's next move is to relate these three types of organization, classified in terms of compliance structure – coercive, utilitarian and normative – to a range of other variables. For instance, one can distinguish between what he calls instrumental and expressive leadership, where instrumental leadership is task related – about getting the job done – whereas expressive leadership is about establishing and representing key values, developing the commitment or engagement of members, and appealing to their convictions. With this distinction, the distribution and types of leadership vary between the three organizational types. Coercive organizations tend to lack leaders of both kinds in the hierarchy, but to throw up expressive leaders among the inmates. Utilitarian organizations tend to fill authority positions with instrumental leaders, with any expressive leaders being restricted to top posts. While normative organizations tend to fill all positions in the hierarchy with expressive leaders.

The propensity for sub-collectivities to develop also varies with the type of organization in terms of compliance structure. By sub-collectivity Etzioni means what, in the parlance of the last chapter, would be called a cohesive informal group with explicit norms, probably hostile to authority. In coercive organizations inmate sub-collectivities are rife; in utilitarian organizations they are less common and milder, but are still present (the famous Bank Wiring Observation Room of the Hawthorne Studies is a fair approximation to a sub-collectivity). In normative organizations, on the other hand, sub-collectivities are rare.

The fact and importance of socialization varies as between the three types of organizations. In coercive organizations there is little official socialization, but socialization in the 'counter-culture' is carried out unofficially in the sub-collectivities dominated by the expressive leaders of the last two paragraphs. Socialization occurs in utilitarian organizations, both official and unofficial, but it is not usually a powerful force. But in normative organizations official socialization is powerful and important (and to a large extent the function of the expressive leaders filling authority positions).

The term 'scope' in Etzioni's work denotes the number and range of activities performed in common in an organization, especially by what Etzioni calls 'lower participants' (inmates, blue-collar workers, or rank-and-file members, as opposed to office-holders in all cases). In coercive organizations the scope is typically high; in utilitarian organizations it is rather low (8.00–5.30 jobs); whereas in normative organizations it is variable (for example, it is low in day schools, but high in boarding schools, low in churches where members simply attend services, meetings and other functions, but high in monasteries and seminaries).

If scope refers to simple activities performed in common, 'pervasiveness' is a stronger term in Etzioni's vocabulary. Pervasiveness is the extent to which activities in the organization, or coming within the organization's purview, are normatively regulated (in the sense of group norms produced in Chapter 4). Etzioni argues that coercive organizations are not pervasive, that is, impose little normative regulation, except unofficially in the sub-collectivities referred to above; utilitarian organizations are also not very pervasive; but normative organizations tend to be highly pervasive, and religious organizations, especially, seek to control the conduct of members even when they are 'off site'.

Patterns of communication differ as between the three types of organization, with little official communication, but some unofficial downward communication by expressive leaders in sub-collectivities. In utilitarian organizations communication tends to be predominantly downward in direction and instrumental by type – it is in the form, that is, of instructions, and job related information. But in normative organizations communication is primarily expressive, and upwards as well as downwards.

'Saliency' is a term Etzioni has adopted to denote the relative emotional significance of organizational membership for lower participants; that is, is membership of the organization emotionally important relative to other activities of the home, private life, leisure kind? Coercive organizations are highly but negatively salient for lower participants (they hate them!); utilitarian organizations tend to have low salience; and normative organizations high and positive salience.

Consensus, or general agreement about means and ends, varies consistently between the three types of organization. In coercive organizations consensus is low, except that there tends to be high 'counter-culture' consensus in the inmate sub-collectivities. In utilitarian organizations Etzioni primly holds consensus to be only moderate (a masterpiece of understatement as attentive readers will appreciate), whereas in normative organizations consensus about activities and their meaning is high.

Even the distribution of charismatic individuals tends to vary as between the three types. In the coercive organizations charismatics are largely absent from official positions, but may emerge in inmate collectivities. Charismatics figure little in utilitarian organizations, except in the ranks of founders or chief executives, but abound in line positions in normative organizations.

We have described Etzioni's ideas at some length, though not exhaustively, because this is a theory which structures the notion of organizational culture in a new way, in terms of commitments, sentiments, styles of leadership and patterns of communication. Or to put it another way, Etzioni's theory relates power, in the form of the compliance structure, to a range of cultural features, many of which have been indicated. Furthermore, the analysis indicates for business organizations what conflict is likely to be about, namely means rather than ends, and it also suggests the values likely to be appealed to in power and policy struggles, those quintessential values of the utilitarian organization – efficiency, profitability and competitiveness.

Culture, structure and gods

Charles Handy, whose definition of culture was quoted at the start of this chapter, is a writer who has not only identified some distinct corporate cultures, and done so very entertainingly, analogizing them with Greek gods[27]; he has also very successfully related culture and structure.

The power culture symbolized by the god Zeus is the first, and its essence is strong central figure – founder, director, or chairman. At its best the power culture is decisive, fast-moving, able to take risks and seize opportunities, though the extent to which these potential strengths are realized depends on the quality and imagination of the central figure. Power cultures are not bureaucratic, rules and procedures are unimportant; personal achievements and relationship with the central figure are what matter and the succession issue is always critical. Power cultures are based on resource power (see Chapter 6). Handy gives as example types smaller entrepreneurial companies, robber baron companies of the nineteenth-century, trading companies, finance companies and some trade unions.

The second type is the role culture symbolized by Apollo, the god of reason. The essence of the role culture is that the overall task is disaggregated into discrete functions and departments – purchasing, engineering, production, and so on. These in turn practise division of labour and maintain strict hierarchy. Roles and procedures are important, and the whole edifice is co-ordinated at the top. Position power is the fulcrum of the operation (see Chapter 6). These role cultures may function efficiently where the organization is well-structured and the environment stable. The role culture of Handy is the mechanistic structure of Burns and Stalker referred to earlier. Handy suggests as examples not only the civil service but also car firms and oil companies (with their long product life-cycles), insurance companies and clearing banks. The strength of the role culture is the ability to act and process rationally and uniformly; its weakness is a limited ability to react to change or challenge, and arguably some frustration for members who are appraised as role incumbents rather than individual political actors in the sense of this book, though role cultures offer a high degree of security instead.

The task culture is Handy's third type of culture and is symbolized by Athena. It is job or project oriented, based on expert competence, and its strength is its adaptability. It aims to bring people and resources together and let them get on with particular tasks. Individual capability rather than age or formal status determines people's standing in the task culture, which has a clear affinity with Burns and Stalker's organic structure. The task culture is appropriate where adaptability is at a premium – where the market is volatile, or the product life short, or where what is offered to the customer depends on several disparate inputs. Handy gives as examples the product groups of marketing departments, consultancies, new venture sections of merchant banks, and account executives in advertising agencies. Control is difficult in the task culture; this is the price paid for fast response and capability.

Dionysus, the god of the self-oriented individual, is the patron deity of Handy's fourth and last type, the person culture. The person culture may be said to exist where the organization exists simply as facilitation and back-up for the 'star performer' individuals. Handy gives barristers' chambers, architects' partnerships, and some consultancy firms as examples, and one might suggest that hospitals and universities with their consultants and professors partake somewhat of the person culture. It is not, however, a culture found in manufacturing companies.

We said at the start that Handy is operating very much on the boundary between culture and structure. This comes out in two ways. First, in characterizing his four cultures he makes substantial use of structural notions: the cultures are actually depicted in terms of organizational arrangements and groupings, most obviously in the case of the role and task cultures. But second, Handy also addresses the problem of why particular organizations evolve these various cultures.[28] His answer is that the choice will be determined by factors such as the history and ownership of the organization, the formal goals, its size and technology, as well as the members who people it and the environment in which it is situated. The interesting thing is that these factors – size, goals, technology and environment – are those generally cited in the literature as the determinants of structure or at least its concomitants. The beguiling thing about the study of structure and culture is that they merge, separate and merge again. They can be distinguished analytically, yet the distinction is often not sustained in the more substantial treatment of the topics. We will add a final dimension by considering a possible relationship between structure and *national* culture.

Structure and national culture

A study conducted at the Laboratoire d'Economie et de Sociologie du Travail at Aix-en-Provence in southern France, generated the idea of the salary hierarchy.[29] A salary hierarchy is the distance between the lowest paid person or group and the highest paid in an enterprise; that is, it is about relativities not absolutes. The study compared salary hierarchies in several companies in France and West Germany and found the French hierarchies to be consistently longer. The gap between the lowest paid labourer and the highest paid top manager, that is, was bigger in the French companies. Not only this, but all the bounded relativities were in the same direction, so that in the French case the salary gaps between skilled and semi-skilled workers, between workers and supervisors, between manual and clerical workers, and between junior and senior management were all bigger than in the German companies.

These surprise findings led the same research institute to a more ambitious study which compared seven pairs of firms in France and West Germany, each pair matched for product and approximate size, with regard to their structure and workforce composition.[30] Again, significant and largely consistent differences emerged. If we take the French companies as the reference point, it emerged that these had longer hierarchies and narrower spans of control, and that they exhibited higher vertical and horizontal compartmentalization. There were more rigid boundaries, that is, between the different functions and departments, and between the different hierarchical levels. The French showed a higher reliance on written communication and on formal meetings. The labour force in the French companies included more indirect workers, that is, more clerical workers and more technical and advisory grades sideways on to production. The personnel in the French companies were also more differentially qualified (had a longer qualification hierarchy!) in the sense of a wider spread of qualifications among the various blue-collar skill grades, and the French firms had managers with higher qualifications on average than their German counterparts.

This pioneering French study introduced a new dimension into thinking about culture. It suggests that national culture is also an influence on structure, alongside size, technology, goals and so on. What is more, these national cultures are likely to contain political and psychological values, which in turn may shape corporate cultures in different countries. In the instance of French and German companies such values would include French educational elitism, German egalitarianism and *Technik*.

It is a pity that there are not more comparative studies of this Franco-German kind. Japan, the only other country whose business cultures have been studied, suggests again a strong patterning of business by society, or of the corporate culture by the national culture.

Climate

We have left till last the idea of climate, which is quite straightforward. Climate is the prevailing ethos; it is what is favoured or disfavoured now, possible or difficult in present circumstances. It is a less substantial and pervasive entity than culture, and it is shorter term.

Climate is often attributed to two particular sources. The first is forces or events outside the organization having some limiting or facilitating effect on the options senior organization members can pursue. The obvious example is the effect on business organizations of the overall economy variously inducing a climate of optimism and expansion or cost-cutting and retrenchment. The second is that the organizational climate is often coloured or changed by powerful figures or groups, so that a new MD or visiting consultant or agents of reorganization after, say, a takeover may have a marked effect on climate. As is argued with examples in Chapter 7, it is quite possible for culture and climate to diverge, at least in the short term.

The political perspective

This section represents a keying in to the political perspective of the discussion of structure and culture and will serve as conclusion to the chapter.

Corporate culture is a highly political phenomenon, in that it affects what people may achieve. It facilitates certain actions and competences, and restrains others. Sometimes it sets limits on what a company may achieve in conventional business terms, sometimes it sustains business success well beyond the ordinary.

As we have seen, culture and structure have numerous possible determinants, many of them impersonal in the sense of being beyond the control of individuals or even dominant coalitions. These include technology, size, and history, and to a large extent the state of the economy and the stability or volatility of the market. But individuals, especially essential leaders, or the organizational charismatics and expressive leaders depicted by Etzioni's theory, will play a role in shaping, sustaining and, above all, changing corporate culture.

In developing the basic idea of the political approach in Chapter 2 we argued that it treats the individual as active, wilful and purposeful. This raises the question: Does the concept of corporate culture sustain the notion of the active individual? The answer is both yes and no. In so far as corporate culture is about shared meanings and accepted values then it is voluntaristic and assertive – it is about what people think, mean and expressively input. At the same time corporate culture is something which confronts individuals, especially as they come fresh to an organization. It is that which may be propounded to newcomers, by word, deed or insinuation. It is that in which new cohorts of organizational members may be socialized. It may shape attitudes and thoughtways, propel some courses of action and restrain others.

We have argued that corporate culture may be important in facilitating or restricting outcomes and choices for companies. It is both possible and desirable to say a little more about where and when it has this importance.

First, corporate culture is both relevant and vulnerable in a takeover situation. A takeover is, among other things, a corporate culture clash. The company which is taken over is likely to experience a reshaping of its corporate culture and this may be the enduring effect after the sensation of the takeover act and the management musical chairs which is likely to follow.

Second, to look at it from the viewpoint of the active partner, corporate culture is quite critical for the success of mergers or acquisitions. If the company acquired is very different in its culture, in the beliefs and assumptions that surround its operation, it will be difficult to merge and manage, and the hoped for gains of acquisition may be dissipated.

Third, corporate culture is probably more important than is generally recognized in determining the success or diversification into new products and operations of the type the company has not engaged in before, whether or not this is done by acquisition. We all know of cigarette firms that have diversified into frozen foods, or telecommunications companies that have gone into hotel and restaurant chains without conspicuous success. These sorts of failures are usually explained in terms of lack of management knowhow, or lack of familiarity with the new product or operations, and the stories of such mistaken ventures are used to justify a 'back to the core business' and 'let's stick to what we know' posture. All this is eminently plausible but it may neglect questions of different and even incompatible cultures associated with different products, markets, and operations. What is going to happen when a building tycoon (power culture) takes over an insurance company (role culture), or when the role culture organization seeks to diversify into task culture operations, say the clearing bank moves into a civil engineering consultancy.

Lastly, the same argument applies to new ventures or departures generally, even if they are not at the diversification–acquisition level. Policy changes, attempts to enter new markets, to serve customers differently, to run a product with a longer life-cycle than the rest, to employ distinctively qualified people in exposed positions, all these are subject to the restriction–facilitation of corporate culture.

Implications for the practising manager

Understanding structure and culture has numerous implications for the individual manager in both defining where he is and developing political orientation.

What kind of situation am I in?

What kind of structure does this company have? (Not just can I draw the organization chart and do I know who reports to whom, but can I characterize it further?) Does it fit the technology as Woodward says? Is it organic or mechanistic? How differentiated is this company? How and how well does it handle intergration? Think of other companies I know – is this one different, and if it acquired the others would it be a seamless garment or a hotchpotch of incompatibilities?

What is the corporate culture here? How well does it handle the exigencies of external adaptation and internal integration?

What is the company philosophy? Is it latent or explicit? Could I meaningfully propound it to an outsider?

Is this company sustaining and transmitting its corporate culture? Is it doing this by symbols and encouraging identification, by expressive leadership, by operational re-emphasis, by selecting the right people to join (or by screening out socio-cultural incompatibility)? Does it socialize new members?

What are the strengths of this culture? What things does it help me to do well?

What are my real goals?

Do I fit the culture? Do I want to accept it, shape it, or change it?

Do I want to do things this structure and culture facilitate, or am I going to have problems?

Do I want to innovate in a tradition and stability culture?

Am I a security lover in a change culture?

Do I like long lead times, long product life-cycles, durable relationships with known customers and plenty of time for planning, or is it the reverse of these things?

What kind of boss do I want? A Zeus or an Appollo? Do I want a boss who uses resource power or position power, or expert power, or personal power? What kind of boss do I want to be, what power base would I comfortably use, and will this corporate culture provide it?

What experience/knowledge to I have to draw on?

Do I understand how this corporate culture developed? Can I identify its strengths and weaknesses in the light of my experience elsewhere?

Does my knowledge and experience help me to see new possibilities within the existing corporate culture?

Have I tried to sustain, share or change a culture before? Did it work? Have I learned from failure? Could I do it better next time?

What alternatives do I have?

Can I do the things I want here, and if not what is the scope for change?

Does the culture structure allow legitimate options that I could use?

Could I set up a counter-culture? Can I shape the thinking and assumptions of those around me?

Can I see powerful people 'acting out of culture' whose cause I would join (or whom it would be tactical to restrain)?

Is the structure here the only one this culture would support?

What impact will different actions have?

Are the strategic options top management is contemplating compatible with our structure and culture? If not, which will change first?

Are things going to happen to this company which will affect the culture?

Is the pursuit of my objectives going to impinge on the system of shared meanings? Will they be good or bad? (For whom?)

References

1 Charles Handy, *Understanding Organisations* (Penguin 1976), p. 176
2 Edgar H. Schein, 'Coming to a new awareness of organisational culture', *Sloan Management Review*, vol. 25, Part 2 (1984), p. 3
3 A.L. Kroeber and Clyde Kluckhohn, *Culture: A Critical Review of Concepts and Definitions* (Vintage Books 1952)
4 Philip Selznick, *TVA and the Grass Roots* (University of California Press 1949)
5 Philip Selznick, *Leadership in Administration* (Evanston, Illinois: Peterson Row 1957)
6 Ian A. Glover, 'Executive career patterns: Britain, France, Germany and Sweden', *Energy World* (December 1976)
7 M. Maurice, F. Sellier and J. Sylvestre, *Production de la Hierarchie dans l'Enterprise: Recherche d'un Effet Social Allemagne–France*, 2 vols, Laboratoire d'Economie et de Sociologie du Travail, Aix-en-Provence, France (1977). For a summary in English, see S.P. Hutton, P.A. Lawrence and J.H. Smith, 'The Recruitment, deployment and status of the mechanical engineer in the German Federal Republic', Report to the Department of Industry, London, 2 vols (1977). Also obtainable from the library of the University of Technology, Loughborough.
8 A. Sorge and M. Warner, 'Variety and determinants of factory organisation in Britain, France and Germany: the United Kingdom National Report',

Report to the Social Science Research Council, London (Autumn 1977).

9   Gareth P. Dyas and Hanz T. Thanheiser, *The Emerging European Enterprise* (Macmillan 1976)

10 M. Panic, *The UK and West German Manufacturing Industry 1965–72* (London: NEDO 1976)

11 Geert H. Hofsteede, *Culture's Consequences* (Sage Publications 1980)

12 Peter Lawrence, *Managers and Management in West Germany* (Croom Helm 1980)

13 Peter Lawrence, 'Swedish management: context and character', Report to the Social Science Research Council, London (1982)

14 Dennis Swann, *Competition and Industrial Policy in the European Community* (Methuen 1983)

15 Anthony G. Athos and Richard Tanner Pascale, *The Art of Japanese Management* (Allen Lane 1982)

16 William G. Ouchi, *Theory Z* (Reading, Mass: Addison-Wesley 1981)

17 Thomas J. Peters and Robert H. Waterman, *In Search of Excellence* New York: Harper and Row 1982

18 Edgar H. Schein, 'The role of the founder in creating organisational culture', *Organisational Dynamics* (Summer 1983)

19 *ibid.*

20 Vijay Sathe, 'Some action implications of corporate culture: a manager's guide to action', *Organisational Dynamics* (Autumn 1983)

21 Alan L. Wilkins, 'The culture audit: a tool for understanding organisations', *Organisational Dynamics* (Autumn 1983)

22 Schein, 'Coming to a new awareness of organisational culture', p. 13

23 P. Lawrence and J.W. Lorsch, *Organisation and Environment* (Harvard University Press 1968).

24 T. Burns and G.M. Stalker, *The Management of Innovations* (Tavistock Publications 1961)

25 For a fuller explanation of Burns and Stalker's theory, with diagrammatic summary, see P.A. Lawrence and R.A. Lee *Insight into Management* (Oxford University Press 1984)

26 Amitai Etzioni, *A Comparative Analysis of Complex Organisations*, (New York: The Free Press 1961)

27 Charles Handy, *Gods of Management* (Pan Books 1979)

28 Handy, *Understanding Organisations*

29 J. J. Sylvestre, 'Industrial wage differentials: a two-way comparison', *International Labour Review*, vol. 110, no. 6 (1971)

30 Maurice, Sellier and Sylvestre, *Production de la Hierarchie dans l'Enterprise*, and Hutton, Lawrence and Smith, 'The recruitment, deployment and status of the mechanical engineer in the German Federal Republic'.

Part Three _____

INFLUENCING BEHAVIOUR

In Part One we outlined the theories of organization which have led to the development of most OB concepts and theories. In Part Two we went on to examine some of the major traditional OB subjects and to show how the political perspective can lead to their reinterpretation and have important implications for the practising manager.

This third part involves the development of a major area of OB which can only be satisfactorily dealt with within a political framework. We focus on the subject of influence. It is true that many modern OB writers are beginning to 'tag on' chapters with headings such as 'Power' and 'The management of change' to their otherwise conventional texts. This is inconsistent because the analysis of these subjects, as we have shown, requires a reassessment of all the facets of OB. Furthermore, the adoption of a mangerialist perspective, even a political managerialist perspective, is very limiting; it tends to lead to the study of 'the use and abuse of power' and 'the functions and dysfunctions of conflict' and 'minimizing the problems of change'.

In the whole of Part Three we shall be concerned primarily with 'how to get your way'. Our perspective is that which we would have if we were the reader of this book pursuing his own goals within an organization rather than a managerialist manager doing what is 'good for the organization'.

6

THE BASES OF POWER AND THEIR PLACE IN THE POLITICAL PROCESS

Outline

This is the first of four chapters focusing primarily on *power*. We shall first review some of the early writings on this fundamental variable and then start to develop a framework which is designed to promote understanding of its major facets and their characteristics. The bases of power, their analysis and the direction of their use, form the foundation of the political framework.

Introduction to power

Most behaviour can be interpreted as political. This point, first made in Chapter 2, is re-emphasized now, as we begin our detailed study of organizational politics, because it is easily lost. Often our examples will focus on people who are trying to compete, to influence decisions, to earn promotion, or to make other changes which might, on first impression, be described as selfish. We use this type of example because it is familiar and exciting. We are aware, however, that people often pursue goals within organizations that they see as primarily beneficial to others. A manager may prevent a colleague from unfairly discriminating against a subordinate. An engineer may threaten to resign if safety procedures are not improved. A personnel manager may fight for fairer bonus payments. Often people pursue positions of power in the belief that their personal honesty and integrity make them right for the job.

The political approach does not favour either selfish or unselfish interpretations of behaviour. It is essentially amoral, not immoral. It could be argued, perhaps, that writing this book and thus helping managers to pursue their goals, whether selfish or not, is itself an immoral position. Our reply is that it is not for us to impose our personal moralities on the reader.

Consider the following scenario:

A young ambitious lecturer decides he wants promotion. He surveys the department in which he has worked for several years and identifies a number of other candidates who are potential rivals. He familiarizes himself with the promotion system and notes that he requires the support of senior colleagues, particularly the head of department, and also that he stands a better chance if he has a good research and publication record.

This is a political situation. Macmillan, whose ideas were outlined in Chapter 3, suggests that our young lecturer will now formulate a political strategy designed to help him achieve promotion. We shall return to help him with this problem later, but first let us try to understand the situation he is in through the variable power.

The basic concept

One of the most quoted definitions of power is that of Dahl: 'A has power over B to the extent that he can get B to do something that B would not otherwise do.'[1] Thus he sees power as a relation among people.

Emerson, on the other hand, defines power in a somewhat 'quantitative' way: 'The power of actor A over actor B is the amount of resistance on the part of B which can be potentially overcome by A.'[2]

The definitions of Dahl and Emerson would help us to think about certain aspects of our hypothetical young lecturer's position. How much power does his head of department have over him and vice versa? What about his senior colleagues? Does he have any power over his rivals? One limitation of these definitions, however, is that they focus only on two-party, dyadic relationships. As Pettigrew says, 'To understand the relative power of A and B one needs to know details of this dyad's relations with ZYX to n. In this way the *power network* or *power structure* is revealed.'[3] Thus, although we may be concerned with power relationships between two people (rivals for promotion, say), we will only be able to interpret such relationships in the light of the wider context of relationships with other organizational members and in the specific context of the promotion decision. One of our young lecturer's rivals may have a close friendship with the head of department, for example, and this may increase his power considerably in the context of a promotion decision.

A second limitation of the Dahl and Emerson definitions is that they require overt behaviour before power can be said to have been exerted. Many political effects, however, may be cognitive rather than behavioural. Handy's definition, whilst still dyadic, helps to overcome this difficulty: 'Power is that which enables A to modify the *attitudes* or behaviour of B.'[4]

This leads to a further criticism of the Dahl and Emerson formula. What if we influence a person's attitudes such that he does not resist – he actually wants to do what we want him to do? By the Dahl and Emerson definitions no power would have been exerted. For example, our lecturer may be convinced by a senior colleague that it is unreasonable to expect promotion at his age. He may thus pursue longer-term strategies, quite voluntarily, but power would have been exerted in the form of attitude change.

So what definition of power would we offer? Clearly it must either be complex, to include a whole range of caveats and provisos or it must be simple. We favour:

Power is the capacity to affect people, things, situations and decisions.

Influence is sometimes defined seperately from power; for it is simply power in operation; power is that which enables us to influence. Influence has the advantage of a verb form which power does not.

Our scenario at the start of the chapter enables us to illustrate some general comments about power. First, power is not a property of an individual. We often say 'he is a powerful man' or 'she is a powerful woman', but these are short forms. What we mean is 'he is powerful in the boardroom', 'she is powerful in cabinet meetings'. We are quite aware that he may have little power on the rugby pitch and she may have little power over her grown-up children.

We are also aware that neither of our characters is 'all powerful' in either the boardroom or the cabinet. With regard to certain decisions, groups of people, individually with less power perhaps, may form coalitions in order to get their way. In some circumstances a single individual, by skilful political manoeuvring, may succeed against the person we see as generally more powerful.

Thus, power is a contingent variable. It depends on the people involved, the situation and the specific decision with which we are concerned. Our lecturer may be very powerful as far as his students are concerned (but even then perhaps only over those who want to pass his exams); he may, however, have far less power to affect the promotion decision.

Power is clearly not a simple phenomenon, it is not one single parameter which we can have a lot or a little of. To understand its nature we must begin to break it down into its component parts, aiming to explore the diversity of things, social processes, attitudes, emotions, circumstances, skills, forces and so on, which may be a part of it. Ultimately we aim to explain their relationships so that the reader can develop his or her facility in political processes.

From our discussion so far it follows that power exists in different forms. Early writers considered the major variable to be the *sources* or *bases* of power.

Sources of power

Dahl states: 'The base of an actor's power consists of all the resources – opportunities, acts, objects, etc. that he can exploit in order to affect the behaviour of another.'(p. 203) If we are to assist the reader in identifying his or her own power then some structured way of thinking about power bases is required. The best known classification of power sources is that of French and Raven.[5] It can be explained by continuing our example of the promotion-hunting young lecturer. What sources of power does a lecturer have? Clearly it depends on the situation. Let us first consider his relationship with a group of committed students:

● They may accept his authority, as the legitimate representative of the college and as a holder of a particular position, to influence their behaviour in certain ways. French and Raven call this *legitimate power*.

- They may recognize his ability to give them good or bad marks. If they are motivated to succeed academically then this ability may give the lecturer power. These are the power bases of *reward* and *coercion*.

- They may like him, they may find his character appealing, they may respect him, and this may lead them to work for him. In an extreme form this may even be hero worship. Such power, based on relationships and character, is known as *referent power*.

- Finally, according to French and Raven, they may respond to the lecturer's influence because they recognize his knowledge and ability and their importance to them. *Expert power* is that which most lecturers would like to think lies behind their influence over students.

The identification by French and Raven in 1959 of these five sources of power represented a major turning point in organization theory. Here, at last, was the recognition that there was much more to getting subordinates to obey than merely having formal authority, as perceived by the classical writers discussed in Chapter 1. Here was an explanation for the fact that often those without formal authority could have power in abundance. Individuals and groups could mobilize different power bases in different ways towards different goals. The basis for a study of political behaviour and conflict in organizations was established.

Progress towards a true political understanding has been, and still is, impeded by the managerialist writers with their desire to be acceptable to managers weaned on classical ideas. This conventional standpoint held that politics was the pursuit of personal rather than organizational goals and conflict was undesirable. This led to a half-hearted and reluctant development of ideas, but inexorably they have moved towards the more radical, pluralist view.

In 1962, David Mechanic studied the power of subordinates in organizations. For him, one has power if one has or controls access to: *information* which people want, *people* who can get things done and/or *instrumentalities*, things that people need or want.[6] This has the merit that it emphasizes control over and access to people. Whereas earlier discussions had tended to relate exclusively to dyadic relationships, Mechanic is also concerned about networks of power.

The sources of power are by no means all-embracing. For example, apart from 'referent power', no attention is paid to the variety of emotional attachments which can provide important power bases. Love, respect, comradeship, loyalty, can all be used to influence behaviour. This is an important area for further research. It is too easy within the political model to forget about deeper social and psychological characteristics and processes. Often we may go along with something we disagree with because of our trust of the decision maker, or we may be too insecure or embarrassed to argue. Group norms and other social forces (see Chapter 4) may affect our behaviour. The political actor can manipulate social and psychological factors in order to help him influence others, but we should note that his own goals and actions are also influenced by such factors.

The fact is that in practice almost anything can be a source of power under the right circumstances. Nevertheless broad categories are useful in order to structure our thought processes.

The basic power equation

Emerson, whose definition of power has been discussed, sees 'dependence' as the basis of all power: 'The dependence of actor A upon actor B is (1) directly proportional to A's motivational investment in goals mediated by B and (2) inversely proportional to the availability of those goals to A outside of the A–B relation' (p. 32). This leads us to the idea that simply possessing resources does not necessarily give us power; they must be important resources to the actor whom we are trying to influence. Furthermore if these resources are available elsewhere then their significance as a power base reduces. This is expressed in a simple equation shown in Figure 22.

This is a general equation which applies to any level of actor – individual, group or organization. Let us illustrate it with a single example. If I have money then I have a resource which could be a useful power base. If money is important to you, that is you need or want it, then I have potential power over you. I may be able to get you to work for me, give me information or, perhaps, co-operation of some other kind. If, however, you have access to other sources of money then my potential power is reduced – depending on the attractiveness of the alternative sources.

The above example relates to individuals. At a more aggregate level, Hickson *et al* studied organizational departments and measured their influence on organizational decisions.[7] They discovered that power tends to be related to (1) the control of resources which are *central* (in our terms 'important') to the work of the organization, (2) the degree of coping with uncertainty (a form of resource) and (3) the substitutability (scarcity) of their activity. This may be a special case of our equation which can be broadly applied to departments, a particular type of coalition. It implies that if one wants to work for a powerful department one should choose an organization in which that department copes with a high level of uncertainty. For example, Marketing in industries which are highly competitive, Personnel in industries with industrial relations problems, and Purchasing in industries with a high level of raw materials costs – particularly where prices are unstable.

Crozier illustrates Hickson's argument with his research in a French tobacco plant.[8] He discovered that the maintenance engineers appeared to possess inordinate power, which they exploited to their advantage. He concluded that this

Figure 22 *The basic power equation*

Basis of Power = F (Resources × Importance × Scarcity)

was largely because the only major unpredictable uncertainty at the plant was machine breakdowns, the rest of production was routine. The engineers kept their irreplaceability level high by, amongst other things, refusing to allow documented repair procedures and by training new engineers verbally.

We noted, in Chapter 3, the research by Pettigrew in which he described the major political strategies of computer programmers in their battle to avert replacement by systems analysts.[9] We saw how they kept control of information and tasks by not keeping records or descriptions and how they tried to create myths about the difficulty of their work and its centrality to the organization.

The fundamental equation expressed in Figure 22 underlies all political processes. Between any two actors there are at least *two* equations operating – the power of A over B and the power of B over A. These equations may be in entirely different terms. For example, parents may have primarily economic power over their renegade daughter; she however may have considerable emotional power over them. The way these two equations operate is an important part of their political interaction – though not all, as we shall see later in this chapter.

Usually there are more than two equations operating. More actors mean more complex possibilities for power bases and networks. Political webs can be woven very intricately indeed. If the renegade daughter has a boyfriend, for example, then her parents may be able to influence her behaviour through him, or even through his parents. In such situations there may be many power bases operating.

Perceived power

The basic power equation is not made up of objectively measurable variables. The resources of an actor, their importance to other actors, and the availability of alternative resources elsewhere, are often highly subjective factors. For example our lecturer may believe he is the best teacher in the department, but if the head of department does not agree, or is simply unaware, or sees teaching ability as unimportant, then the power base may not be high.

It is this 'unknown' aspect of many of the variables in a political situation which makes the development of political insight and skill so valuable. If an actor can build up people's perceptions of his qualities and their value, he can increase his power base without changing the qualities themselves.

Frequently people are unaware of their own resources and importance; they perceive themselves as powerless. This can be a self-fulfilling perception. There are also those who overestimate their power bases and they too may pay a political price.

The hardest part of the equation to establish is 'importance'. Often we know that an actor wants something from us but we can only guess how much. This may lead to a negotiating situation in which the parties 'feel their way' to an agreement.

'Negotiation' is sometimes taught as part of an Industrial Relations course, as though it applies exclusively to formal union/management relationships. In fact we all negotiate regularly as part of our daily lives. Consider the following examples:

> A young child did not want to get his hair cut. His father had threatened him with punishment in the past but decided to try new tactics. 'If you get your hair cut regularly I'll increase your pocket money to 40p.' After some haggling they settled on 50p provided the son helped with washing the car!

> The dividing fence between two properties was the legal responsibility of one house owner but he knew that his neighbour was keen to have a fence of a particular type. Negotiation led to them splitting the cost 50:50 and building the specific fence the neighbour desired.

Negotiating is a political art which will be discussed in more detail in Chapter 9. At this stage, however, we should note that uncertainty over the variables in the power equation is one of the major reasons why skill is so important. The ability to bluff, to create the perception in the other party that you are at your limit and will make no further concessions, is essential. You must also be able to read your opponent's bluff – sensitivity skills again (see Chapter 3). In the examples above the child was uncertain how much his father wanted him to have his hair cut, and the house owner did not know how much his neighbour wanted to influence the type of fence. The compromises reached were a function of both the facts of the situation and the negotiating skills of the parties.

Potential power

The basic power equation is further complicated because sometimes actors choose not to use particular power bases. For example a well built subordinate may disagree with his diminutive supervisor but is unlikely to use his physical strength to help him get his way. Quite apart from long-term negative consequences, the subordinate may simply not consider the use of such power, or, if he does, may reject it as illegitimate.

Failure to recognize a power base, or refusal to use it, are thus factors which ensure that potential power is not converted into action. Our ambitious lecturer may be aware that one of his rivals is having domestic problems – his children are in trouble with the police. This could be useful ammunition in the battle for promotion but only if his principles allow him to use it.

Involuntary power

Sometimes a power base may operate without the user being aware of it. For example a supervisor may ask a subordinate to perform some non-work task on the basis, as he sees it, of personal friendship. The subordinate may agree to do the task, however, for fear of some reprisal (a bad appraisal perhaps) if he refuses.

It is important for the political actor to be aware of his own power bases. These may operate whether or not he wants them to. The subordinate in the above example may become resentful of what appears to him an illegitimate use of power – with possible negative consequences in the long term.

Choice of power bases

Usually, political actors have a choice of which power base or bases they will mobilize in order to achieve given objectives. In our haircut example earlier, the father chose between coercion and reward. An industrial supervisor often has choices such as between threat, reward, appeals to loyalty or friendship and legitimate authority. He will tend to resort to similar power bases consistently and this is an important element in his leadership style (see Chapter 3).

Vital questions to ask here concern the side-effects and the aftermath of political behaviour. Certain power bases may have undesirable consequences. Resorting to threat 'Do it or you'll get an official warning' may make the wielder unpopular; it emphasizes power difference and may build up resentment. The constant use of reward – 'Get your hair cut and I'll give you 40p' – may lead to the expectation that rewards will always be forthcoming. The use of legitimate authority – 'I'm the boss, what I say goes' – emphasizes status differences and may lead to subordinates doing what their job description requires and no more. The use of emotional ties – 'Please do it for me, out of friendship' – may lead to reciprocal demands on the same basis. And so on. Choice of power base and also the method of application are vital political considerations. We shall return to this theme later when we focus more explicitly on the mobilization of power in Chapter 8.

Contextual power

The definitions of power discussed at the start of this chapter do not alert us to one major element in the political situation. By focusing exclusively on the relationship between actors they may blind us to the importance of the context within which they are acting. This may have considerable influence on the nature and consequences of their actions. Figure 23 represents a simplified view of our promotion example.

The power equations of all the actors will be affected by a range of contextual factors such as, in the hypothetical case of our example, the nature of the promotion system – does it favour those with good research records or those with teaching skills? Also the formal hierarchy is important – giving senior staff and the head of department special status, and so on. Much influence is being exerted in this situation by the context itself. Some aspects of the context are in fact political tools of actors who are not represented in Figure 23. Someone, or more likely some coalition, established the promotion system and the organization structure to try to ensure that they would mould people's behaviour in line with their objectives. These actors are easy to overlook in a political analysis which just concentrates on

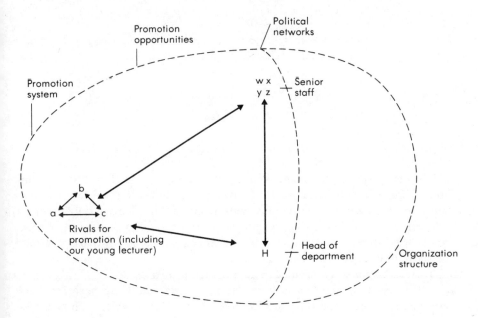

Figure 23   *Politics and promotion*

overt behaviour and obvious relationships. However the effect of their 'rules', 'systems', 'structures' and other forces may be highly significant. Clearly, political context must have a place in any comprehensive political framework. This is the subject of Chapter 7.

The direction of power

So far we have discussed sources of power and their position in the basic power equation. Determination of the power basis for each actor in a political situation has been shown to be problematic for a number of reasons:

- The factors in the equation are complex and hard to establish, this is true for resources, importance and scarcity.

- Even with relatively small numbers of actors the quantity of variables becomes large.

- There are differences of perception between the actors.

- The distinction between potential and actual power must be made.

- Sometimes the use of power is involuntary.

If we add to this the fact that people and circumstances are continually changing, we can see why political behaviour will always be more craft than science.

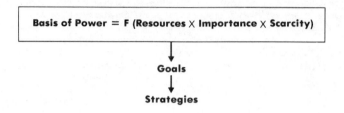

Figure 24   *The direction of power*

The next step we must make is to incorporate some idea of *direction*. I know something about a political rival if I have assessed his power bases, but I know much more if I am also aware of his goals. Even this knowledge is only partial, it tells me where he is heading but not how he proposes to get there. Of equal importance to me is information about the strategies he proposes to use. I need to be aware of both ends and means.

This development of our ideas is represented in Figure 24.

In Chapter 3 when we looked at 'motivation' we were studying the forces which affect human behaviour. It is true that there are many forces which are intangible – group pressures, emotional bonds and so on – it is also true that these forces affect people differently because of variations in personality, beliefs and circumstances. At the end of the day we have made the simplifying assumption that, in a great many situations, people are goal directed. That is, they are positively trying to do something.

Often it is easier to establish the goals an individual is pursuing than the reasons why he is pursuing them. It may be clear that a colleague is a rival for promotion, or is simply after a quiet life until retirement, or is very committed to the purchase of a new machine. Insight into the reasons behind particular goals *may* be useful politically. It may offer strategic possibilities for removing those reasons or for creating counter-pressures to change the goals.

Organizational and individual goals

There is a management control system known as Management By Objectives, or MBO, which is built on this assumption and which has enjoyed some success. The system, first popularized by Drucker, involves an attempt by the top management to impose a cycle of goals on the organization.[10] Goals are established at the top for the organization as a whole and the major functions. These are divided into sub-goals which are discussed and agreed with managers at the next level down the hierarchy. In theory each manager may, in conjunction with his superior, modify the goals if they are inappropriate. He must develop detailed working plans to show how the set goals will be achieved. This process continues down the hierarchy. The modified goals then pass back up the hierarchy to provide a new set for top management. If the modifications are felt to be undesirable then this problem is tackled by another flow of discussion and, theoretically, agreement down the hierarchy.

MBO is intended to be a way of life rather than a control system. At the end of, say, six months, a review of progress is carried out, failures are explained and new goals and plans made. The idea is that the manager will make the agreed goals his own and will thus be highly motivated to achieve them. If he succeeds, his personal satisfaction will be high and he will have contributed to organizational goal fulfilment.

In practice the basic principles underlying MBO are found in many organizations, even where the system is not formally applied. It is the embodiment of managerialism. It has also had some major failures. Levinson, a notable critic, identifies the reasons.[11] The system fails to answer questions such as:

1 What are the manager's personal goals?
2 How do they change from year to year?
3 What relevance do 'organizational goals' and his part in them have to his personal needs and wants?

Within our framework, we would expect the system to operate most harmoniously where consensus is high and/or where the power of the top management to impose goals without question is great. In organizations where goals are heterogeneous and power is dispersed we would expect to find that a formal MBO system merely provides a focal point for disagreements, a political battleground in fact.

Organizations do not have goals, only people do. Nevertheless it is clear that organization members often believe that their organization does or should have goals. Where there is a high level of agreement over these goals, harmony is possible. Walsh *et al* note 'Genuine agreement on the goals and values of an organization may be a limiting case, but it is a possibility that should not be ruled out.'[12] However they also emphasize 'Genuine value consensus does not exclude differences of interest. Acceptance of overarching values for the organization does not mean that there will not be differences over how resources should be distributed(p. 141).' In other words, even if we agree over ends we may still disagree over means. This helps to explain much political behaviour within organizations even where the members accept managerialist goals. The same logic, of course, applies to any political situation; even though two actors may concur about what they are trying to do, they may battle seriously over how they should set about it.

It is often important for the political actor to be aware of managerialist goals and the way his goals and strategies relate to them. It is frequently necessary to argue that actions which are personally beneficial are also desirable in managerialist terms, that is 'good for the organization.' The climate of many organizations is such that overt pursuit of goals which run counter to those which are commonly held to be acceptable will meet resistance.

Strategies

In pursuit of their goals people adopt strategies – this is the essence of the political model. Many people see themselves as 'non-political'. This may mean that they simply do everything other people tell them without question. Few people who are capable of reading this book would accept that their behaviour is explained in this way.

Others may call themselves non-political because they believe that they are pursuing organizational goals. 'Politician' is a criticism directed at those who pursue activities which are not compatible with the goals that our non-politician believes are appropriate.

A third category have simply never had their eyes opened to the political pressures on them and have never thought in terms such as 'how to get my way'. They have been manoeuvring for most of their lives but are only now coming to realize it. Chapter 8 is an analysis of the process of strategy formulation which should be interesting to them.

Summary

To draw together the major points made in this chapter we shall return to our ambitious young lecturer in pursuit of promotion. We could, of course, as easily have chosen a sales executive or an Inland Revenue inspector or a bank manager. We chose a lecturer because most of the readers of this book will be students and they may enjoy some insight, albeit oversimplified, into their lecturers' political milieu.

Similarly, we need not have chosen the promotion process for the political scenario, it could have been the introduction of a new machine, a recruitment decision, a disciplinary problem or any of the infinite possibilities. Promotion, however, is often one of the more dynamically political situations and, in our organizations, one which interests most people.

In this chapter our young lecturer has learned that all the actors in the promotion process have resources which they may use to influence events. Different actors possess different resources and he will need to learn as much as he can about them, the qualifications and allies of his rivals, the access to the decision process of his senior colleagues, and the multiple resources of his head of department. He has learned that these resources have different effects and values in different situations, so he must relate them to the specific context of his department and the promotion decision.

It should now be possible to establish the power bases of each actor, bearing in mind that some resources are more important than others and some are more significant, owing to their scarcity. Confidence in his calculations may be reduced, however, because of the different perceptions of his colleagues of the power bases concerned. Can he obtain information on this? Who is well thought of? What are the key criteria for promotion?

He has learned of the need to identify the goals of the different actors with respect to the promotion process. Who are his rivals? Who is concerned with helping whom? Is there a view about what the department needs in terms of senior lecturers which may influence the decision process?

Two final and major factors have been briefly touched upon. The context of the political process has been shown to have a bearing on political activity. In terms of our example, the context is the number of senior lectureships available and the allocation of key roles in the decision process. Context will be the subject of Chapter 7. The strategies which may be chosen by the different actors will cause our subject much concern; he will perhaps be more competent to understand and manoeuvre when he has read Chapters 8 and 9.

References
1   R.A. Dahl, 'The concept of power', *Behavioural Science*, vol. 2 (1957), pp. 201–18
2   R.E. Emerson, 'Power-dependence relations', *American Sociological Review*, vol. 27 (1962) pp. 31–42
3   A. Pettigrew, *The Politics of Organizational Decision-Making* (Tavistock 1973)
4   C. Handy, *Understanding Organizations* (Penguin 1976)
5   J.R.P. French and B. Raven, 'The bases of social power', from: D. Cartwright (ed.), *Studies in Social Power* (Ann Arbor: Michigan Institute for Social Research 1959)
6   D. Mechanic, 'Sources of power of lower participants in complex organizations', *Administrative Science Quarterly*, vol. 7 (1962), pp. 349–64
7   D. Hickson, C. Hinings, C. Lee, R. Schmeck and J. Pennings 'A strategic contingencies theory of intraorganizational power', *Administrative Science Quarterly*, **16**, (1971), pp. 216–19
8   M. Crozier, *The Bureaucratic Phenomenon* (University of Chicago Press 1964)
9   Pettigrew, *The Politics of Organizational Decision-Making*
10 P. Drucker, *The Practice of Management* (New York: Harper and Brothers 1954)
11 H. Levinson, 'Management by whose objectives?', *Harvard Business Review*, vol. 48, no. 4 (July–August 1970), pp. 125–34
12 K. Walsh *et al*, 'Power and advantage in organizations', *Organization Studies* (1981), 2/2: pp. 131–52

7

THE CONTEXT OF THE POLITICAL PROCESS

In this chapter we focus on the context within which political processes take place. We identify the factors which make up the political context and the ways in which they affect, indeed are often part of, political activity. This enables us to complete our framework for understanding the political process.

Introduction to political context

Consider the following scenario:

> ABC Distilleries of Scotland have just taken over the PQR Brewery of Yorkshire. John McMillan, a successful young manager at one of ABC's distilleries, has been transferred to PQR as chief accountant, in order to introduce a range of new management accounting systems. This is seen as essential by the ABC management since it was failure in this area which made PQR vulnerable to takeover despite many product and marketing strengths.

We can make a number of political statements on the basis of this scenario:

- The *circumstances* which led to PQR's takeover included management accounting weaknesses.

- New management accounting *systems* would provide ABC management with information about the performance of PQR managers. They would include targets, budgets and standards by which PQR managers could be assessed.

- John McMillan belongs to an important *political network*, the ABC management.

- Chief accountant is a senior position in the *organization structure*.

Any political actions which McMillan takes will be very much affected by the four considerations above. None of the statements is about sources of power, not directly at least, but the statements clearly cannot be ignored in a political analysis of McMillan's position. They are part of the *political context* into which he is moving.

His senior position in the organization structure will give him legitimate authority over many people in PQR as well as access to information and other resources. The circumstances of PQR's failure, which have led to McMillan's arrival, could affect people's reactions – will they see the need for change, resent his presence, fear him? Backing from the ABC political network will provide significant real power bases if required, but it may be that the mere perception of this potential power will suffice to influence most people. Finally, the change which he is to bring about is a system change. Systems affect all our lives. When they are carefully monitored, and enforced by important rewards or sanctions, they are impossible to ignore. If McMillan successfully introduces new systems, he will be affecting the behaviour of many people in PQR for years to come. This will have been achieved not by influencing them directly through sources of power but by manipulating their political context.

The political context has a large number of aspects which the actor will need to understand. The following list is not exhaustive:

Circumstances
Systems
Networks
Structure
Culture
Climate
Norms
Agendas
Socialization

These contextual factors provide the framework for this chapter. Each will be discussed in turn to provide insights into its importance and characteristics. The reader is asked to try continually to relate our analysis to his or her own situation; this is possible even in a college environment. Few people are fully conscious of the impact of the political context on their lives and it is only by crossing the gap from our exposition to his or her personal experience that a true appreciation is possible.

Circumstances

Circumstances include a very wide range of factors which may provide opportunities, apply pressures or create threats for the political actor.

If a firm is growing rapidly there is more chance of achieving promotion or getting approval for high risk projects. If there is a decline in demand for a particular product, this may lead to pressures for new product development, criticisms of the marketing manager, or perhaps a cost-cutting exercise. If a law is passed which makes advertising a particular product more difficult, then this threat may lead to new marketing strategies.

It is clearly important for the political actor to be aware of existing and future circumstances in order not to miss opportunities, to be able to respond quickly to possible threats, to meet new challenges and to cope with constraints. Anything and everything *may* be important; technological developments, new products, proposed restructuring, availability of funds, colleagues' future plans and so on.

The circumstances of business organizations in the UK include its essentially capitalistic economy. It has been argued by some writers that this provides such powerful constraints on the business that freedom of choice by decision makers within it is considerably reduced.[1] Thus if managers choose to make decisions which are inefficient, unproductive or expensive in managerialist terms then their organizations will become uncompetitive. They will then either be put out of business, or taken over, or will be forced to make managerialist actions to restore competitiveness.

This argument is not without merit. The economic and political environment applies powerful pressures to decision makers which must not be underestimated. The same type of logic applies to the work of Woodward, Lawrence and Lorsch and the other contingency theorists discussed in Chapter 2. They emphasize the importance of technological and market environments as influences on organizational change. These factors are major forces but they do not *determine decisions*, they only *affect decision makers*.

For most managers the majority of their activities has only a marginal effect on organizational performance. They can choose from a range of alternatives (all with uncertain outcomes) and not be called to account in managerialist terms.

Systems

Systems include job descriptions, rules, procedures, routines, policies and other prescribed ways of behaving. Most organizations abound with such devices: appraisal systems, job evaluation systems, payment systems, decision-making systems, planning systems, hours systems, – the list is almost endless.

Often the individual cannot affect these systems, he has to operate within them. If, for instance, a production manager wants to buy a new machine then he must justify his plan to the Capital Expenditure Committee, working within his budget and to the required financial criteria. If a supervisor wants to dismiss a subordinate he must go through the formal procedure laid down in industrial relations legislation and company policy for the particular dismissal grounds. If an employee has a grievance he must raise it through the formal grievance procedure. However, even the most powerful system rarely operates absolutely as it is designed.

It *may* be possible to by-pass a system, or corrupt its effects with false information or by influencing the people who operate it. This is an important point for the manager to note. There are many examples: most managers 'pad out' their financial budgets to allow for contingencies and to give them some margin for manoeuvre; it is not unheard of for employees on incentive schemes to ignore safety regulations which slow down production; in an emergency a manager may by-pass the purchasing department to obtain parts which will keep the line going.

However the system will, under most circumstances, affect people's behaviour.

It is common for managers to turn a blind eye to occasional lateness, or to ignore transgressions by valued colleagues; nevertheless the very act of *not* applying a system is different in character from the same behaviour if the system was not there. For example, in return for overlooking lateness the manager might expect flexibility about overtime; for overlooking rule-breaking he may exact some favour in return. Once the system is in existence it is likely to become a major political force.

Organizational systems are usually designed by, or for, particular interest groups in order to promote the fulfilment of their objectives. These interest groups tend to be most interested in productivity, return on investment, profitability, market share and other managerialist goals. This helps to give economic organizations their distinctive characteristic and was discussed in Chapter 2 as a powerful stabilizing force, preventing too much overt conflict.

Networks

Networks of relationships in organizations and the types of groups which may exist were discussed in Chapter 4. Let us here simply emphasize their importance by drawing on an example:

> Sue joined her present company when she graduated. She has been with them for eight years, three of them in her present department – Industrial Relations. Before that she worked in Personnel and before that she was with Work Study. The company employs over 3000 people but Sue feels a part of it, she has been well rewarded for her hard work over the years and knows she is well thought of at higher levels. Also, whilst Sue does not know everyone, there are few places she can go in the company where she does not have friends or at least acquaintances.
>
> Sue belongs to a large number of coalitions and has a very wide network of relationships. They are, in her opinion, both essential for her to do her job, and important to her career prospects.

Let us emphasize the extent of Sue's personal network. The first coalition she joined was the company itself. At that point she tied her prospects, to some extent, to the company's development. At the same time she joined the Work Study department, another coalition. Her commitment here was weakened by the fact that she saw this as a stepping stone, but she worked hard and in return received a promotion and transfer to Personnel.

Her colleagues, friends and acquaintances in Work Study now changed in political significance. Some became providers, or potential providers, of information. Some, closer in relationship, were trusted confidants. Some became potential allies in situations where cross-departmental relationships were valuable.

As time passed and Sue's career progressed, so did those of many of her earlier colleagues. They reached positions where they were more likely to come into contact and were more able to exert influence on each other's behalf.

Furthermore, Sue's achievements came to the attention of higher level managers and she did what she could to increase her reputation, volunteering for projects which would be highly visible. In this way she could ensure that all the messages being received by higher managers showed that Sue was very keen to support their values and join their coalitions.

The political importance of networks is enormous. People can rarely bring about change on their own. By combining together with others they can increase their potential to influence events in two ways – by drawing on each other's power bases and by working together on the strategy formulation process.

Coalitions are sometimes like-minded people pursuing the same objective. Often, however, people come together because they can pursue separate ends by the same means – as, for example, when a change in package design will be supported by the distribution manager for its easier handling properties and the accountant for its lower materials cost. A related point concerns people who ally themselves to coalitions in pursuit of their own objectives, even though they may not support those of the coalition. An example of this is the consultant who produces a report recommending the proposals of the managing director irrespective of the facts of the situation. The consultant wants his fee and any future business.

Coalitions may also be formed on an exchange basis. Managers often act in support of a colleague in return for support on some issue of their own. Sometimes the return will not be negotiated at the time of the initial act – 'a favour sown is a favour reaped'.

Structure, culture and climate

These aspects of the political context have been discussed in detail in Chapter 5. Here it is sufficient to restate their significance with some emphasis.

One of the authors, in a study of promotion processes at a distribution company,[2] discovered the change in *structure* illustrated in Figure 25.

When the branch manager left, instead of replacing him, the managing director decided to restructure the branch so that a junior commercial manager took over that side of the business and a salesman was placed in charge of the sales team –

Figure 25   *Structural change*

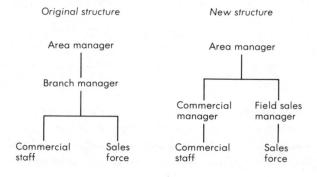

both reporting to the area manager. Both these incumbents had hoped for branch managership and were disappointed. However it was made quite clear to them that the possibility was still open if they performed well. It is clear who has exerted most influence over future activity at the branch.

The importance of organization *culture* can be re-emphasized by considering the position of workers at the Matsushita plant in Japan:

'Each person is asked at least once every other month to give a ten minute talk to his group on the firm's values and its relationship to society. It is said that nothing is so powerful in persuading oneself as having to persuade others. Matsushita has long employed this technique of "self-indoctrination". Subordinates may be asked to consider a proposal they have set forth in light of the values of Matsushita . . .

1) National Service through Industry
2) Fairness
3) Harmony and Co-operation
4) Struggle for Betterment
5) Courtesy and Humility
6) Adjustment and Assimilation
7) Gratitude'[3]

This quote gives us an idea of both the culture at Matsushita and the deliberate manner of its inculcation. In most British companies culture is less positively created but its impact on behaviour is still great.

Climate is related to many other contextual variables. Culture is a significant part of climate but it is more enduring and less immediate in its effects; one can often realistically wait for a change in climate but to wait for a change in culture would be hopeful. The following discussion demonstrates this relationship:

Production manager   The new machines have to be introduced as soon as possible, we need to cut costs and keep up our good delivery record.

Accountant   I'm all for cutting costs but at the moment that would mean spending money we don't have. You'll have to make do with the old machines for another year.

Personnel manager   This would be a bad time to make radical changes. We're involved in wage negotiations which are both complex and sensitive. If we announce plans to introduce new machines now it would give the unions a powerful lever.

Managing director   The overriding short-term problem is liquidity, we have to generate more cash. Measures are in hand to improve the situation and I think I can promise you that new capital investments will be feasible within six months, by then things should be quieter on the industrial relations front.

The cultural elements of this scenario are below the surface – the support for managerialist goals. These four managers are clearly playing for the same team even though their positions are different. The cultural factors support the need for the new machines. The climate, however, is not so favourable, cash is short, wage negotations are under way. Here we see once again the political impact of contextual factors rather than people.

Norms

Norms were also discussed in Chapter 4. These patterns of accepted behaviour can be influenced by skilful political activity but they are ignored at any actor's peril. Consider the case of Mike Deane:

> Mike Deane took over as supervisor from Tim Blake. Blake had always been successful, he had a relaxed leadership style but his subordinates liked and respected him. One obvious manifestation of Tim's lax discipline was that he allowed people to drift away early at the start of the month when things were slack. In return everyone worked hard and at month end when there was too much to do no-one demurred at the considerable unpaid overtime.
>
> When Mike arrived he was insecure, it was his first supervisory position. He clamped down hard when people tried to leave early. He saw this behaviour as an attempt to test his authority. By the end of the month, output was down and no-one would work overtime to meet the deadlines.

Mike had not realized the importance of norms nor taken sufficient time to read both sides of this one.

Agendas

The political 'agenda' is the range of issues which are currently the subject of overt activity. If something is not a part of this agenda is it politically important?

At this point in our analysis we are about to extend our appreciation of power beyond that provided at the start of Chapter 6. Up to now we have thought of power primarily as the ability to *do* things: to make decisions, to take actions and to make others take actions. Two writers, Bachrach and Baratz, point out that there is a tendency to overlook the considerable power which may be unobtrusively wielded in what they have called 'nondecision-making'.[4]

Nondecision-making they define as 'the practice of limiting the scope of actual decision-making to "safe" issues by manipulating the dominant community values, myths, and political institutions and procedures' (p. 632). This idea can be made clear with a number of examples:

- If managers hold all their resource allocation discussions in terms such as 'profitability' or 'productivity' because they dare not voice their sectional objectives, since they are politically unacceptable, then the party(ies) who create this climate are exerting nondecision-making power. The parties may be their colleagues with whom they are dealing as well as those at the top of the management hierarchy.

- If a manager who controls the agenda for a meeting decides not to put a certain item on it because he believes the outcome of discussion will go against him, he is exerting nondecision-making power.

- If management refuses to allow unions to be involved in key issues such as job design, promotions, dividends, pricing, and so on, because they want to keep their prerogatives, that is nondecision-making power.

- If a manager learns about a new technology, pay system or some other change but decides not to examine the idea in case the outcome does not favour him, he is nondecision-making.

- If a leader chooses not to allow his followers to participate in many of the decisions he makes, in other words he adopts an autocratic style, then he is nondecision-making.

Preventing issues from surfacing, modifying the political agenda, can be a major use of power. It is not overt or obvious and for this reason may be hard to detect and counteract.

Socialization

Continuing to develop our concept of power, and at the same time our awareness of the political context, we must now explore the importance of socialization.

Socialization is, in sociological terms, the process by which individuals are influenced by the society in which they live and are raised, and come to accept certain norms and values. It is the accumulated influences of parents, schooling, friends, community, the media, and all the other aspects of society, on our beliefs and values. From cradle to grave no-one can escape from it. Socialization is a never ending process and one of the important arenas in which it takes place is at work.

The employee has been long prepared for his work experience. He has been taught to accept authority all his life, his parents', his teachers' and now his managers'. He has been encouraged to adopt the basic values of his society: the rights of ownership, work for pay, achievement for promotion and so on. These beliefs provide a framework within which he perceives the specific socializing forces of his peers, his department and the organization. Often, particularly in the UK, these forces will work partly against one another, there will be competing pressures and loyalties which will be interpreted by the individual depending on his previous conditioning and his personality.

Stephen Lukes is a writer who has developed strong ideas on this subject.[5] He calls Dahl's focus on observable behaviour and conflict the *first dimension* of power. Bachrach and Baratz's identification of suppressed nondecisions and covert conflict he calls the *second dimension*. This he sees as still inadequate because it assumes 'if men *feel* no grievances, then they have no interests that are harmed by the use of power.' (p. 24). The *third dimension* is the process of influencing people's attitudes, beliefs and values.

' "A" may exercise power over "B" by getting him to do what he does not want to do, but he also exercises power over him by influencing, shaping or determining his very wants.' (p. 23). We can see the force of Lukes' views: 'Is it not the most insidious exercise of power to prevent people, to whatever degree, from having grievances by shaping their perceptions, cognitions and preferences in such a way that they accept their role in the existing order of things . . .' (p. 24)

The difficult part of Lukes' argument for many to accept stems from this last quote. He distinguishes between 'subjective' interests of the actor, and 'real' or 'objective' interests, perceived by the observer, and thus between observable conflict, where subjective interests are involved, and latent conflict, where real interests are involved.

The problem here is that observers are not objective people, they have their own values and beliefs which will bias their perception. A marxist observer will see latent conflict in every business organization, as the employee works to make profit for the owners; a capitalist observer would not perceive this as conflict. It will be necessary for every researcher reporting on the basis of 3D power to tell the reader about his own values so that his observations can be interpreted in that light.

Nevertheless the concept is a vital one. We are all influenced by our environment. Why do we accept our boss's right to give us orders? Why do we accept managerial prerogatives to decide such matters as capital expenditure, pricing policy, dividends and political party contributions? Is it not because we have been conditioned to believe such issues are the right of managers to decide?

Operationally, the concept of socialization is important too. Organizations provide managers with a range of ways to influence people's minds – induction and training programmes, employee handbooks, policy statements, company journals and all the variables which affect organization culture. For those who want to be managers one day, there are norms to follow, values to accept and a range of behaviours to be adopted if one is to fit the mould.

Top managements in some organizations work very hard at influencing employees, attempting to instil a company philosophy. In the IBM handbook there are five pages expounding 'company beliefs' incorporating such headings as:

IBM means service
Respect for the individual
Superior performance
Pursuit of excellence

Contextual influence

Having examined the major features of the political context, we can now show how they relate to other political factors, resources, goals and strategies, which were introduced in Chapter 6. Socialization, and the other aspects of the political context – norms, agendas, culture, structure, systems and so on – provide a considerable array of influences on the individuals who work in the organization. These influences specify the 'rules of the game' by which the ordinary actor must usually play.

Figure 26 represents the process of contextual influence within the full political framework. This shows the actor, individual or group, with his power base. The actor is pursuing goals with selected political strategies. Because organizational resources are scarce and because actors conflict in terms of goals and the means to

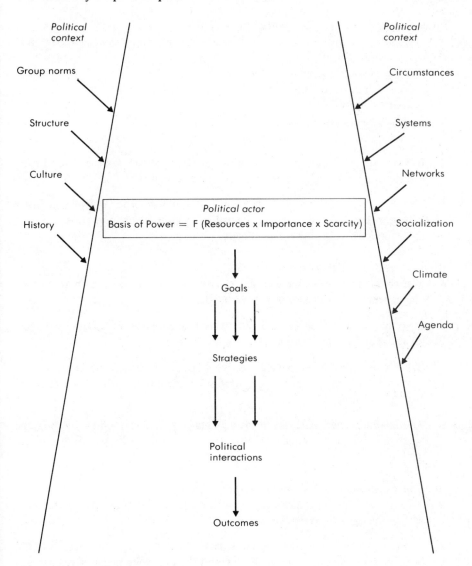

Figure 26 *Framework for understanding political activity*

achieve them, political interactions take place. These result in outcomes which, in practice, would feed back into all the other features of Figure 26 and affect future political action.

The political context surrounds all aspects of the political process. Each contextual factor may affect the actors' power bases, the goals they pursue, the strategies they adopt, the nature of the political interactions which result and their outcomes. We shall illustrate these relationships by enumerating a range of examples.

Power bases and the political context

- If a manager is appointed to a particular postition in the *organization structure* that may give him:
    perceived authority
    access to information
    access to people
    ability to reward/coerce
    status

- If there are two people in a department with a particular essential skill and one leaves, this *circumstance* may increase the power of the other.

- If the employees in an organization have all been *socialized* into believing their managers have the right to make decisions and impose changes, this increases the effectiveness of 'formal' authority.

Goals and the political context

- Managers may be influenced by *systems* in their organization to pursue managerial goals in order to achieve goals.

- Employees may be *socialized* or 'motivated' to believe they should work hard for the 'good of the comapny'.

- *Group norms* may develop which lead to sectional identification, restriction of output, loyalty to the supervisor, or other characteristics which influence the goals people decide to pursue.

- The *climate*, particularly in terms of what is politically achievable, may be taken into account by individuals, often subconsciously, when developing personal goals.

Strategies and the political context

- An actor may be forced to adopt strategies in pursuit of his goals, which are within the existing *systems*.

- Some strategies may not be considered because they conflict with the prevailing organization *culture* and would thus provoke negative reactions.

- The *socialization* process may cause some strategies to be rejected as unethical.

Political interactions and the political context

- *Organization Structure* may mean that two subordinates cannot fight their battle with each other but must go through their bosses.

- Particular decision-making *systems* such as committees, working parties and consensus groups will affect the types of interaction which can take place between actors.

● Strong *group norms* may mean that arguments must be presented in terms of their advantages for the group rather than in terms of their advantages for the actor.

Conclusion

In this chapter we have examined the major aspects of the political context within which those of us who work in organizations have to survive. We have shown how each of these aspects can often influence the behaviour of organization members even without personal reinforcement by those who created them in the first place.

Finally, we have examined, using examples, the mechanisms by which context influences action.

It is clear from the points made above that the context of a political process will have a major inpact on its outcomes. This leads to a vital conclusion: *There is much power in being able to affect the political context*, often more, and with longer-term effects, than possessing strong power bases and adopting effective strategies *within* the context. The strategic implications of this will be examined in Chapter 8.

References
1   R.L. Morris, *The Economic Theory of 'Managerial' Capitalism* (Macmillan 1964)
2   R.A. Lee and H. Crowhurst, 'Advancement – theory and practice', unpublished research report, Dept. of Management Studies, Loughorough University (1984)
3   R. Pascale and A. Athos, *The Art of Japanese Management* (Penguin 1982)
4   P. Bachrach and M. Baratz, 'Decision and nondecisions; an analytical framework', *American Political Science Review*, vol. 57 (1963), pp. 632–42
5   S. Lukes, *Power, A radical View* (Macmillan 1974)

8

POLITICAL STRATEGY

Drawing on the political framework which has been developed in preceding chapters we will now begin to examine the processes of political strategy formulation and execution. We will first look at the prescriptive advice on 'how to succeed' which is available. Then we will look at different types of strategy and their potential outcomes. Finally, we will develop some methods for improving strategy formulation.

Introducing strategy

By and large, managers with more knowledge, more useful allies, more authority and more resources will win out in political battles with those who are ill informed, isolated, and without authority or resources. This general statement, whilst undoubtedly true, is unhelpful to the political actor. He needs to understand the specific considerations he must make to help him with his real, one-off, political situation.

Consider two opponents in a chess game. When the game starts they have equal power bases – the pieces, their positions, quantities and capabilities (resources, scarcity and importance). As the game progresses the power bases change. Often it is difficult to assess who is winning, one player may sacrifice pieces for position, the game may ebb and flow from one player to another. What determines who wins? It cannot be the power bases of the two parties, these were equal at the start. Furthermore, it is possible for a player to take over a game in a weak position and still win. The determining factor is *strategy*.

Strategy is not merely about the use of power bases, it is about their development and about their mobilization in the light of others' strategies. Politics is never a solitary activity and each interaction has both a past and a future.

In the chess game each player knows the other is trying to win. In life, however, actors have to develop their own goals and assess those of others, both of which may be difficult processes. Even if goals are obvious there is usually a range of potential strategies, which can be directed at them. Sometimes multiple strategies can be followed, complicating the matter further.

A number of strategies may serve equally well to achieve the actor's goals but he will also need to consider other issues:

How much risk is attached?
Will my ethical beliefs allow me?
What side-effects may occur?
What will be the aftermath?

Each strategy must be developed on the basis of imperfect answers to some of these questions and imperfect knowledge of what other people will do.

Political interaction

Figure 27 represents the involvement of a number of actors in a political process. These might be departments competing for resources, directors arguing over policy, or colleagues trying to avoid an unpleasant job; in essence the processes are the same.

Each actor has power bases which have been conferred by the context or developed by the actor during past political activities. Increasing power bases for future use is a common type of political action.

Each actor has a personal perception of the situation and personal goals and values. These too will be influenced by the context and past activities. The perception of the situation will include some estimate of the other actors' positions.

Each actor will develop personal strategies directed at his goals. These will lead to specific behaviour (or lack of it) which culminates in political interaction.

Major issues are rarely resolved quickly; they may never be resolved. Nevertheless any or all of the factors in Figure 27 will eventually change, often the passage of time is enough. Actors continually reassess the situation, their goals and their strategies. Thus the political story unfolds. It is more complicated than this of course. Actors are involved in many issues at the same time, often the issues are interrelated. If two actors are involved in more than one common issue then the strategic opportunities may be considerably widened; deals, exchanges, pressures and counter pressures become more likely.

Strategic prescriptions

Many writers on organizational politics, instead of considering the subject of strategy in depth, merely prescribe for the reader a range of strategic possibilities which are felt to be helpful. This is the simplest approach to strategy and a good place to start our explorations.

One of the earliest examples of this type was written by Martin and Sims in 1956.[1] They recommend such activities as:

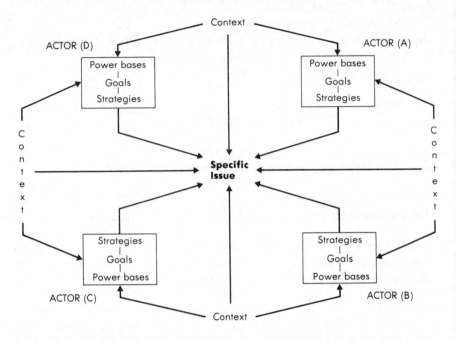

Figure 27 *Political interaction*

- Involving others in decisions only when you need them, thus keeping a close grip on what happens around you.

- Forming sponsor-protegé relationships. Sponsors can provide channels for advancement while protegés make loyal followers.

- Never completely committing to any one position or programme in case external forces require a change of direction.

- Learning when to withhold information or time its release to maximum advantage.

- Developing an outward appearance of confidence.

- Avoiding close friendships from which you cannot withdraw if the situation demands.

A more recent example in a similar vein is given by Hunt.[2] He adds to the list ideas such as:

- Acquiring the expertise the organization requires – preferably in advance.

- Join the leading department, and not one which is in decline.

- Acquiring the values, attitudes, and behaviour codes of those with power.

- Performing well at your job.

- Wining and dining those with power, and even

- Using one's family to 'multiply one's impact on the organization'!

The reader who is interested in more such advice should refer to Farnsworth,[3] Parkinson[4] or Webster[5] – in all cases the authors of lively and very readable books. But there are no books in this genre to match Niccolo Machiavelli, whose experiences of, and perceptions about, sixteenth century Italian politics were synthesized into his classic work, *The Prince*.[6] Many of his brilliant observations and maxims are as relevant today as they were almost 500 years ago. The reader can hardly help but be shocked by his treatment of political issues. For Machiaevelli it is the relationship between means and ends which matters, not the underlying ethics. He in fact goes beyond the neutral position of this book to discuss what a political actor should do to achieve ends which are hard to defend morally, by means which would be impossible to justify in any ethical argument.

In practice, of course, the simple prescriptions of all these writers, even Machiavelli, can only be useful if the circumstances are right. They can all be shown to relate to our political model and involve using its properties. For the manager facing his unique, personal problem, however, they are oversimple. What he needs is help in understanding the situation and then help to develop a suitable strategy. It is hoped that in the preceding chapters he has already learned much which will help him with both these processes. There is more to come.

Types of strategy

A more advanced way of thinking about political strategies which may be used in organizations is to classify them into particular types of behaviour. If we can group individual strategies into a limited number of categories with similar characteristics then perhaps it will be possible to explore the effects of those characteristics rather than the infinite range of individual strategies.

We shall consider five types:

Push strategies
Pull strategies
Persuasion strategies
Preventive strategies
Preparatory strategies

Push strategies
A father who beats his child in order to make him obey, a manager who threatens dismissal for poor performance, and a group of workers who restrict output in order to get improved working conditions are all using strategies with a similar underlying character. We shall call this group 'push' strategies because the actor

on whom they impinge feels a force pushing or pressurizing him to change his behaviour.

Push strategies often rely on coercive power, sometimes directly, sometimes indirectly. Kipnis *et al*,[7] in two studies concerned with influence tactics in the work situation, identify three major push behaviours:

1 'Assertiveness', which includes actions such as continually checking up, giving orders, setting deadlines, 'bawling out', and enforcing rules.
2 'Sanctions' which include preventing pay rises, threatening job security, and threatening loss of promotion.
3 'Blocking', which includes threatening to stop co-operating, engaging in work slowdowns and applying social forces.

The dangers which are associated with these types of tactics are their potential for eliciting unpredictable emotional responses and negative after-effects. 'Push' pressures, if too overt, can be seen as illegitimate by the recipient, he may feel resentful or his pride may be hurt. Futhermore he may feel a need to make a stand, even if it is unsuccessful, in order to prevent further such treatment – if you stand up to the school bully once he may leave you alone the next time.

Pull Strategies

Pull strategies involve providing positive forces to influence behaviour. Much modern motivation theory, as outlined in Chapter 3 is concerned with commending strategies of this type to the supervisor.

By providing opportunities for recognition, achievement, advancement and other needs or goals to be satisfied if others will perform in ways that we want, we may well be able to exert influence successfully. Futhermore, such strategies, particularly when followed by formal superiors, are likely to be seen as legitimate and will not produce negative reactions.

Offering more money or some other tangible reward for the desired behaviour is the most obvious pull strategy. Some are less obvious. With young children we praise them when they do well at something, partly so that they will continue to do well and learn particular patterns of behaviour. The reward here is emotional, most people prefer to be liked, respected or in some way well thought of. Forces such as these can be exceptionally important in social groupings. They have a 'push' side too; how often do we avoid doing things because they would upset or offend people whose sensibilities we are concerned about?

Handy[8] emphasizes the 'invisible but felt pull' of personal magnetism or charisma. Some people can instil in others a desire to please, to be loyal, to follow, simply because of their personality. We have all met highly charismatic individuals, of course, but in general this is a force which most people can mobilize only over particular individuals. It requires considerable skill to influence others in this way with no back up mechanisms based on other power sources.

Persuasion Strategies

Under this heading we may group a range of strategies which involve either 'give and take' or attempts to change the attitudes/beliefs/values of the other party.

Pure persuasion, using no push or pull, would rely on logical reasoning to convince the other party that his behaviour is not appropriate for achieving his goals. More often, however, persuasion is simply a vehicle for transporting a subtly disguised mixture of push and pull:

Manager John, it would be most helpful if you would take over the alpha project.

John But, I'm fully loaded at the moment.

Manager Well, I'll approve overtime of course. There is no-one else in the department who could make a decent job of it. You're the man with the experience and proven ability – as I said to the managing director only yesterday.

Has John been persuaded by pure reason? More likely he will respond to the 'pulls' of overtime pay, recognition and the maintenance of his image with higher management. This last factor, of course, carries an element of 'push' too – when you cease to be well thought of, your prospects are dim.

Kipnis *et al* identified a range of persuasion possibilities, including:

Writing plans to justify ideas. Presenting only information which favours the desired outcome. Demonstrating competence before making requests.

Sometimes persuasion involves exchange or compromise. The subject of negotiating to achieve the best outcome is dealt with in more detail in the next chapter. At this point, however, we may note that such strategies are especially useful when all parties have some power and when there is a need to maintain a relationship after the interaction. Usually, though not always, all parties can go away with something and the aftermath should not involve bitterness – certainly less than when overt push strategies are used.

Exchanges may be quite open, as when management seeks increased productivity in return for a pay rise or when an employee offers to show a junior colleague how to complete a difficult project in return for assistance with some mundane task. But often they are less obvious and less contractual, for example when a subordinate works very hard for his boss in the expectation of promotion – he may be unsure whether his boss will acknowledge both sides of the arrangement but he has to see it through.

Also to be included in this category of influence strategies are those which involve not just immediate persuasion over some issue but changes of fundamental attitudes, beliefs and values. Use of propaganda, training and other methods of social conditioning are common in business organizations. On an interpersonal level it is quite possible to change a person's way of thinking, perhaps with no short-term aim in mind but with a view to achieving long-term behaviour modifications. In general 'push' and 'pull' strategies have to be maintained or repeated in order to stay effective (and often their effects diminish with use), whereas once a person's mind has been changed the effects can last for life.

Preventive strategies

Here we are primarily emphasising the ideas of Bachrach and Baratz outlined in the previous chapter. Sometimes it is possible to prevent an issue from ever arising, perhaps by excluding it from an agenda, or by not raising it when others are unaware, or by distracting attention elsewhere.

A related strategy is concerned with delaying tactics. Managers frequently receive instructions they do not wish to follow and find ingenious ways to avoid doing so. A colleague relates his method for dealing with such instructions:

> 'I note the date on which they are first received – and do nothing. In most cases the originator forgets. If, however, he follows up, I note the second date and do nothing. At the third occasion I compare the gaps between the first and second, and second and third dates. If they are increasing I know the originator's commitment is waning, if narrowing, then I must take some other action.'

Dangerous with major issues, of course, but there are many variations on this theme.

Preparatory strategies

The final category of strategies we will look at is those which are specifically concerned with creating the right environment for other strategies to be more successful. The simplest examples involve such behaviour as:

● Acting in a friendly manner prior to asking for something.

● Praising someone, building up his ego, before setting him a challenging task.

● Waiting for the right moment, when other forces are favourable, before asking for a rise.

All the processes by which we create impressions of ourselves in other people's minds can be included here. Doing a good job, dressing smartly, being enthusiastic, adopting a relaxed leadership style – all such aspects of our work lives are preparation for future influence attempts.

Finally, although this is a potentially enormous category, we should note that managers are often in a position to create situations which favour themselves: meetings can be held in the manager's office; he can have subordinates prepare information reports; he can decide who should be present and so on. Such advantages are very likely to give him the upper hand.

Factors such as seating arrangements in meetings and the selecting and ordering of items on an agenda may not at first seem significant but the experienced manager knows how vital they are. He will fight to be involved in these processes if he really has some vital matter to raise. If he can, he may prime allies and attempt to disarm opponents before the meeting starts.

Multiple strategies

Most influence attempts involve more than one strategy. How does a supervisor get his subordinates to work harder? More pay, recognition or promotion perhaps, if they perform well, but if they do not, an array of negative possibilities – discipline, transfer or merely being overlooked for advancement. The carrot *and* the stick, pull and push. The lecturer who praises his students for their past efforts, then tells them how vital this subject is to their future careers, and finally offers a bottle of wine for the best piece of coursework is using multiple strategies. Furthermore, he is backed up by the way the students have been socialized to want to learn and succeed, and by the system which makes coursework marks count towards exams, and also by the importance of qualifications for later career opportunities.

Contingent factors

So far in this chapter we have only helped the strategist by identifying possibilities – different broad categories of strategic behaviour. We have noted that 'push' is more likely to have negative side-effects, and subtlety is generally to be preferred. The next step must be to examine in more detail what factors affect the efficacy of particular options. Kipnis *et al* provide the following suggestions:

1 Nature of influencer's goals
2 Status of target (influencee)

In other words, what you are trying to achieve and who you are trying to influence. They identify five types of goal:

Obtain assistance on own job
Assign work
Obtain personal benefits
Initiate change
Improve target's job performance.

The three types of target are subordinate, co-worker and superior.

Their findings make sensible reading. As target status increases they find persuasion tactics more widely used. Push tactics are rarely used on superiors. Push tactics are common when assigning work and trying to improve performance; persuasion is also much used for this latter purpose but more when trying to initiate change.

Most research in this area is concerned with the special cases when a superior is seeking to improve subordinate performance and/or satisfaction. It would be superfluous to repeat here the contents of Chapter 3 but we should note that if these are your goals then 'motivation' and 'leadership' are important areas to study.

Clearly much more research into the effects of different types of political strategy in different situations is required. A more developed list of possible contingent factors can be drawn from Figures 26 and 27. Different strategies will have different efficacy depending on:

● All the contextual factors discussed in Chapter 7.

● The particular power base of the actor.

● The actor's goals.

● The power bases, goals and strategies of the other actors involved.

For the student it may be helpful to identify strategic possibilities and make generalizations about their outcomes. These have similar value to theories of motivation and leadership. However, the practising manager dealing with his unique situation needs knowledge of a different kind; the gap from general to specific is a large one. In other human relations areas the emphasis has now moved from theories to skills, particularly sensitivity and adaptability training, so that the manager can learn to diagnose situations and respond appropriately. These are vital skills for all political behaviour.

There are, however, two intervening stages between general theory and unique practice which can be helpful. First, it is possible to analyse specific, common, political situations in detail. If the manager encounters such situations then he will be better equipped to handle them. Secondly, it is possible to develop *processes* for analysing political situations and formulating strategies, which can be used in a wide variety of situations.

In the next chapter we shall adopt the first approach and examine three specific types of political situation – the negotiating situation, the decision-making situation and the interpersonal situation. The remainder of this chapter, however, will be devoted to a general explanation of ways in which better strategies can be developed.

Strategy formulation processes

What we are trying to do in this speculative discussion is to suggest procedures and devices which can be helpful to the political actor. Many situations will not warrant detailed consideration and others will demand action too quickly for effective planning. Nevertheless the ideas presented may be useful, if only to stimulate political thought processes.

In order to illustrate the argument, we will refer to the following scenario:

David Pedlar is the product development manager of Excel Bicycles Ltd. He and his team have been testing new designs, one of which will replace the aging 'Blockbuster' bicycle which is losing its place in the market at an alarming rate. No-one in Excel questions the need for a new product, but there are differences of opinion about the potential replacements.

Don Saddler, the production manager, and Michael Frame, the chief accountant, favour the 'Dambuster' design, which is a direct descendant of the 'Blockbuster'. Its main advantages are that it will be an easy and low cost transition to the new product. There will be less expenditure on retooling and retraining than for the major alternative design.

David himself, and John Spoke, the marketing manager, would prefer to adopt the highly innovative 'Starlight' model. They feel that the additional costs of the changeover would be well worth the investment.

Political strategy formulation must start with two activities, the development of explicit goals and an assessment of the current situation.

People often do not have clear goals. They have a rough direction at the back of their minds, a broad picture of where they would like to go and what they would prefer to happen. But they are not specific about details. If they are to stimulate action, goals must be measurable.

Goals will be more effective if they take the form, 'I will double my output by June', than if they are expressed fuzzily, thus, 'I will do more'. The first goal has quantity and time scale; it is possible to succeed or to fail. The second goal applies much less personal stimulus.

> David Pedlar is quite clear about his goals. He intends to make sure that the 'Starlight' model is adopted. He also has some subsidiary goals, in particular he does not want to upset either Saddler or Frame because they will be key figures in the success of 'Starlight'. Also, David often has to work with them on other aspects of his job.

Goals are inevitably formulated at the same time as the political context is being assessed. There is no point in setting goals which are clearly impossible, owing to contextual constraints, although it is a matter of personal choice whether we set simple or difficult goals.

When considering the context it is necessary to analyse all the aspects described in Chapter 7 and represented in Figure 26.

> David is aware that the final decision about the new model will be made by the managing director, Helen Bell. However, Bell will consult all four senior managers and would prefer them to arrive at an agreement among themselves.
>
> There are no formal authority or status differences between the four men. Their past actions provide no reason to doubt their commitment to the financial success of Excel. The working atmosphere of Excel is very much one of independent specialists managing their separate functions, collaborating only when essential.

For most people the analysis of context is more hazy than it needs to be. Although the picture can never be complete, there are some devices which can help. One such device, the actor/issue matrix is shown in Figure 28.

Even a rough identification of the key issues you are concerned about and the parts different actors may play in them can be useful. For each issue ask yourself who is likely to be for, against, neutral or indifferent, with respect to your goals. Also what power do they have to influence events?

This matrix, as with the others we shall recommend, can only stimulate ideas, show links between factors and help ensure consideration of all aspects of the problem. In practice we have found that all but the simplest situations would

Possible political actors

		A	B	C	D
	a				
Key issues	b				
	c				

Figure 28   *Actor/issue matrix*

require large matrices with overwhelming numbers of variables. It is the fact that the relationships represented by the matrix exist which is important. Usually it is unnecessary to explore *all* the possibilities. In our scenario we shall outline the essential points rather than drawing matrices.

David is clear in his mind about the respective positions of Saddler, Frame, Spoke and Bell on the new product issue. There are other issues on the political agenda, however, which may be important.

Spoke, David's closest ally, has been offered a job by a rival company. He is young and highly ambitious, searching for new challenges. Helen Bell does not want to lose her marketing manager, especially to a competitor.

A major issue over the last few months has been a possible takeover by one of their suppliers, the huge engineering conglomerate Pipe Investments Ltd. Excel's poor performance but still robust financial status and useful physical resources make it an attractive prospect. David himself is not averse to the takeover, but fears that, without a good reason to the contrary, all cycle production would be stopped in favour of other Pipe Investment projects.

Another helpful idea may be the relationships matrix shown in Figure 29. In each of the boxes you can try to identify the nature of relationships between actors. Who are allies? Who are enemies? Who has regular contact? What networks of power exist?

An alliance on the new product issue has been formed between David Peddlar and John Spoke. They have discussed the matter several times and are strongly

Figure 29   *Relationships matrix*

Political actors	A	B	C
A	X		
B		X	
C			X

convinced of their position. Saddler and Frame, whilst both in favour of the 'Dambuster' rather than the 'Starlight', rarely see eye to eye on other matters. Saddler regards Frame as the major barrier between himself and an efficient factory filled with gleaming robots and other modern technology.

Helen Bell, the managing director, tends to hold herself aloof from the day to day relationships between senior managers, but David believes her confidence in Saddler is lower than that in himself and Spoke. Michael Frame, the old accountant, has long been her close friend and confidant, perhaps partly because she knows he has no ambitions to progress beyond his present position and is totally committed to Excel's future.

It is, of course, necessary to make some assessment of the goals and potential strategies of other actors. Figure 30 an ends/means matrix may help with such deliberations.

Whilst in broad terms, all the actors are trying to improve the market and financial performance of Excel, there are differences between them which David sees as important.

Saddler has been complaining for years about the lack of modern equipment in his factory. He claims that, in recent months, only the drop in orders has allowed him to carry out sufficient maintenance to keep operating at all.

Frame has grave doubts about Saddler's ability and this is one reason why he does not favour a radical product change.

Spoke, the marketing manager, sees himself as a 'high flier' surrounded by ultra-conservative colleagues. He has a good record of success which he wishes to add to, not just for Excel's benefit, but also to further his own career.

Helen Bell has had a broad management background, which made her the ideal choice for managing director when she was appointed just two years ago.

Figure 30 *Ends/means matrix*

Key actors	Probable goals	Means to achieving goals
A		1 2 3
B		
C		

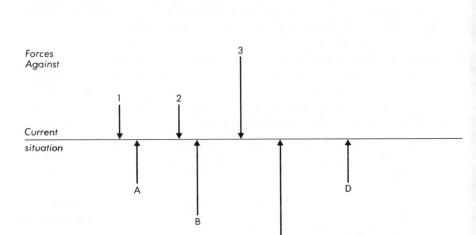

Figure 31   *Force field analysis*

She has been learning about the company and its people and has already made a number of major improvements. This is the make or break issue for her and David believes that anyone who opposes her final decision will not survive long with Excel. She will have to make the decision effective and cannot risk less than total commitment amongst senior managers.

Building on these devices, the political actor can hopefully represent his problem on a force field diagram, as shown in Figure 31. This is probably the single most helpful device for the political strategist. In its simplest form it involves a five stage process:

1 Define the target situation and the current situation.
2 List the forces (people, environment, system) for and against the achievement of the target.
3 Evaluate the forces by describing them qualitatively and noting any relationships between them.
4 Represent the forces on a force field diagram, perhaps using a scale from 1 to 5.
5 Consider the opportunities for improving existing favourable forces and reducing unfavourable forces. Can new positive forces be introduced?

It must be admitted that in practice even these simple devices can become unwieldy owing to the sheer quantity of data involved in all but the most simple situations. They can, nevertheless, stimulate more complete analysis than would otherwise be carried out. Perhaps their imperfections indicate that politics will always be more art than science!

The force field diagram has already moved us into a consideration of ways of changing the current situation in our favour. It is important to generate alternative strategies. We have already discussed different categories of behaviour and these may help bring out ideas. Be inventive, there are always more options than you think. Be systematic, tackle each aspect of the context and each actor involved. What counter strategies may be used by others?

Different alternatives must be evaluated against goals. Once again, this process usually has to be carried out with imperfect information. Sometimes it is possible to represent each option on a different force field diagram for comparison purposes. As part of the evaluation it is important to assess the sensitivity of alternatives. What is assumed, guessed or based on questionable information? What changes may occur and with what consequences?

Assessing side-effects and aftermath are also part of the evaluation process. Try to be aware of *all* the outcomes of your strategy.

David Pedlar has now assessed the situation and is considering a range of strategic possibilities in pursuit of the 'Starlight' new product option. A simple force field analysis is represented by Figure 32. This has been annotated to reflect some of David's considerations.

Hopefully, the reader can generate some strategies which David might follow. He may try to persuade both Saddler and Frame that the best, perhaps the only, way to avoid a takeover is to take the extra-risk 'Starlight' option with its potentially greater return. It may be possible to convince Saddler that his best chance of getting new machinery rests in the more innovative option.

A powerful weapon for Pedlar would be some *information*. His ally, Spoke, could do some market research and, he would hope, produce a report showing that sales of 'Starlight' would be considerably above those of 'Dambuster'. The figures will play an important part in this decision but predicted unit costs depend very much on predicted sales – this is where the data battle must be fought.

On a more subtle level, there is a major strategic option. Can Pedlar exploit the gap between Saddler and Frame? Saddler is a far less important ally, he does not have the confidence of the managing director. It may be possible to isolate him completely and win over the accountant. Perhaps Frame would lean towards an opportunity to discredit Saddler for personal reasons, but this is more likely if they are supported by clear professional arguments from Pedlar and Spoke. If it is pointed out to him that Saddler's life expectancy with the company is likely to be short if 'Starlight' is adopted against his wishes, then this unfortunate fact may be justified in Frame's mind as 'best for Excel'.

This has been a simple example. In reality the strategist would need to consider not only his own actions but also the potential actions and responses of all the other actors. Also it is sometimes possible to change course in mid stream. Some strategies are more flexible than others and allow manoeuvre if their outcomes are undesirable.

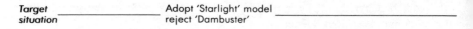

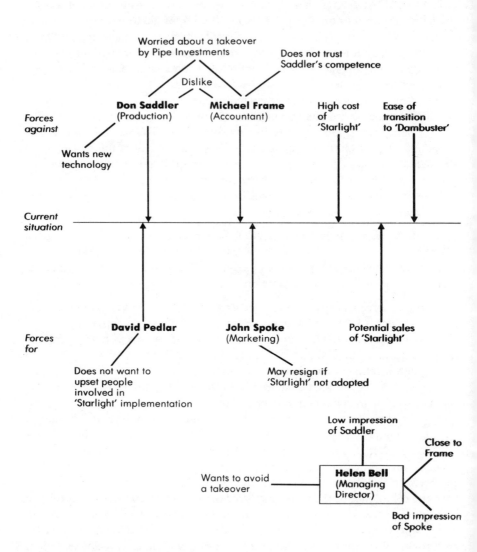

Figure 32   *Force field analysis: Excel Ltd*

The general ideas about the strategy formulation process which we have explored in this chapter are a tentative contribution to an area in great need of further study. In the next chapter we shall explore some common types of strategic situation which researchers have already begun to open up.

References

1 N.H. Martin and J.H. Sims, 'Power tactics', *Harvard Business Review* (November–December 1956)

2 J. Hunt, *Managing People at Work* (Pan 1979)

3 T. Farnsworth, *Managing for Success: The Farnsworth Formulas* (McGraw-Hill 1981)

4 C.N. Parkinson, *In-Laws and Outlaws* (John Murray 1964)

5 E. Webster, *How to Win the Business Battle* (Penguin 1967)

6 N. Machiavelli, *The Prince* (Penguin 1961)

7 D. Kipnis, S. Schmidt and I. Wilkinson, 'Intraorganizational influence tactics: explorations in getting one's way', *Journal of Applied Psychology*, vol. 65, no. 4 (1980), pp. 440–52

8 C. Handy, *Understanding Organizations* (Penguin 1981)

9

POLITICAL SITUATIONS

In this final chapter on influencing behaviour we will continue to focus on political strategy. Three common political situations will be discussed in order both to develop understanding of them, and to suggest effective ways of behaving when they are encountered. They are: the negotiating situation, the decision-making situation and the interpersonal situation.

The negotiating situation

The following are not negotiating situations:

- A car salesman is determined to get £5000 for the blue saloon car on the forecourt; he will not accept a penny less. The customer has offered £4500 and refuses to spend more.

- A father has told his daughter to be home by ten. She says 'Can't I stay out longer?' He replies 'Oh, all right then, but be back by midnight.'

- A man complains about his neighbour's weeds which are unsightly and encroaching on his garden. The neighbour says 'Yes, I'm concerned, but can't seem to get rid of them.'

The first scenario may originally have been a negotiation but is now a deadlock. Negotiation will not produce an outcome if both parties are serious about their commitment. The second case is simply submission by the father. He has expressed concern but has received nothing from his daughter; there has been no compromise. In the third situation the neighbours have a joint desire to remove the weeds, and they should be able to work something out; this will be a joint problem-solving exercise rather than a negotiation.

The following *are* negotiating situations:

- A customer is interested in buying a particular car if the price is right; the salesman is keen to sell.

- A father tells his daughter to be home by ten. She says 'If I promise to stay home and help with lunch tomorrow, can I stay out until midnight?' He replies 'All right, provided there are no more late nights this week.'

- A man complains about his neighbour's weeds and the neighbour says 'Yes, you have a point, but that overhanging tree of yours is a nuisance to me.'

What are the main differences? In the second set of scenarios the participants have conflicting goals; they cannot achieve them without some movement by the other party and there is, we hope, a desire to compromise.

Negotiation, then, is a means of resolving conflict, which applies under certain circumstances. From the political actor's point of view it is essential to understand this process because of its prevalence and because negotiating skills can significantly affect the outcomes. Figure 33 represents a simple situation involving two parties: The two actors, A and B, may be negotiating about one or a number of issues. Each actor has some 'break point' beyond which he will not go, these are the

Figure 33   *The negotiating process*

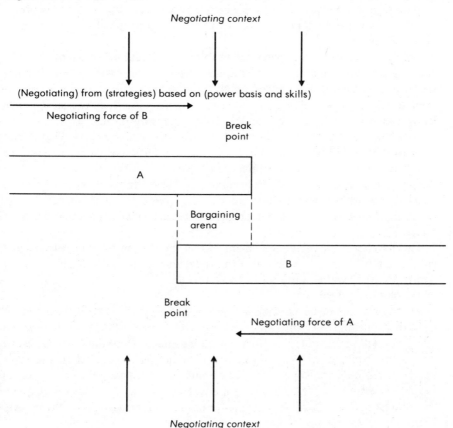

things he considers he *must* get from the negotiation process. The other limit of the continua cannot be stated because no-one knows what is the best deal they can expect.

The interactions take place within a particular context. The important considerations here are exactly those discussed in the last chapter. In formal negotiations, past history is often a major factor. The parties have established patterns of behaviour and expectations of each other. This can lead to accepted rituals concerning such matters as the size of the opening claim and the type of response given, and the postures taken at various stages in the process. Fisher[1] emphasizes the immediate 'atmosphere' of negotiations as important; a climate of trust, friendliness, integrity and frankness all promote acceptable outcomes. Their lack may make solutions impossible despite mutual need.

The negotiating context may confer different power bases on the actors. In times of high unemployment, trade union representatives' power may be weakened, but if the new employer has full order books with fast approaching deadlines, this may change matters. If a salesman knows that he represents the only supplier of a vital raw material, then his position in price negotiations is strong. If a subordinate knows it would take six months to train a replacement, then his chances of negotiating a wage increase are good. Thus, in terms of power bases as well as context, negotiation involves the same type of analysis as other political processes.

Figure 33 shows that each party will be influenced by the other to move from its opening position towards the bargaining arena. Where, within this arena, a settlement is reached will depend on both the political forces available to each actor and the skills with which they are used. Before discussing negotiating skills, let us make some more general remarks based on the diagram.

First, the important variables are all unknown, at least to one party. They do not know each other's break points, nor strategies, nor interpretations of context. This makes negotiation a particularly uncertain process, perhaps it explains why we, in the western world, prefer not to negotiate in many situations where it can be avoided. We are prepared to sacrifice a good deal for secure knowedge. In any event, the lack of hard facts is what makes the essence of all negotiation the art of bluff.

Second, there can be no agreement unless there is an overlap between the continua. Unfortunately, when we start to negotiate we often do not know if there is an overlap and we certainly do not know its extent. There is a clear need for skills in exploration and probing.

Third, there can be no agreement unless one, or more likely both, parties move from their opening positions. Negotiation involves give and take. In general, no one party will move unless it obtains some movement from the other in return – to do so would seem weak negotiation. The aim is to pour oil on the other party's continuum whilst pouring glue on one's own, dragging the other party as deeply as possible into the bargaining arena. How do we do it? We shall explore this central question later. Meanwhile we need to know more about the process itself.

Stages in negotiation

All negotiations involve five main stages:

Prepare
Discuss
Propose
Bargain
Close

Prepare

Frank and Jim were both involved in projects which required the use of the departmental computer. There had been endless arguments between them on the many occasions when they had held each other up. A meeting was planned for tomorrow to discuss the situation.

Frank just turned up.

Jim, a more experienced negotiator, spent some time preparing for the meeting. He decided what he wanted to achieve and what he thought Frank wanted to achieve. He found out as much as he could about Frank's project. He thought out his opening stance and the arguments he would use to defend it. He also decided, in advance, the concessions he would reluctantly make to keep Frank happy.

Who is likely to achieve the best compromise?

It seems obvious to advise negotiators to prepare *before* confronting the other party(ies), yet in practice few people do. The simplest preparation procedure involves:

Set goals: Decide those which it is *essential* you achieve and those which are *desirable*.

Assess opposition: Put yourself in their shoes. What goals would you set? How would you see the situation? What strategies would you follow?

Compare goals: Start to think in terms of 'trades'; remember the aim is to get the best compromise, not achieve a crushing victory.

Develop strategy: What will be your opening position? How will you argue your case? How will you achieve concessions and only slowly give ground yourself?

Allocate roles: If there are other people involved then make sure that not everyone talks. Someone may take notes, someone else may question opposition arguments, but, in general, one main negotiator is best.

Discuss

Frank's early inputs to the negotiation were of four main types:

'Hello, how's the family?'
'I'm glad we've got together for a chat, it's a nuisance this shortage of facilities.'

and

'How do you feel about earning some overtime by using the machine in the evenings?'
'What priority does your project have in the department's annual plan?'

and

'I see the situation like this . . .'
'We ought to have time allocations related to the importance of the project.'

and

'I'd prefer to work overtime in the evenings but weekends are also possible.'

The discussion stage of negotiation often starts with an *opening* phase in which the aim is to reduce tension. So much of the process involves uncertainty that stress may be very high at the outset. It is too easy to be tempted into argument or debate, leading to sarcasm and point scoring. In general, it pays to find ways to settle emotions before starting business. The main function of discussion, however, is to map out the pitch on which the game will be played. *Questioning* will be used to gather information, clarify the position and test the commitment of the other party. It will also, of course, be necessary to state how you see the issue. Finally, the negotiator should watch for, and make, *signals*. These involve indicating that you are prepared to move on particular issues, provided the right concessions are made.

Propose

Jim   We obviously need to use the computer out of normal hours.
Frank   I agree. Look, if you are prepared to do your overtime during the week, I'll do mine on Saturdays, provided we can reach agreement on who should be allocated different times during the week.

The aim here is to move towards the bargaining arena. Different aspects of the negotiation should be subject to tentative offers or claims. The formula to follow is 'If . . . then . . .'

'*If* you can meet the following conditions . . . *then* I might be prepared to . . .'

It is also necessary, under many circumstances, to give reasons for not giving a lot of ground. This is part of the act of bluff which is discussed later.

Inexperienced negotiators try to move too fast at this stage. Forcing the pace can raise tensions and often involves blind guessing about the other party. It is also too easy to throw concessions about without getting a return. It is usually wise not to reject offers instantly, but to build on them, or seek justification for them and question it.

Now is the time to refer back to your preparation. How do the proposals match up to your 'essential' and 'desirable' goals? How are your strategies going? Do you need to ask for an adjournment so that you can think things through again? It is tempting to reformulate goals and strategy 'on your feet'. This is a hazardous practice, especially against a skilled negotiator. Car salesmen, for example, are masters at building up enthusiasm in the customer, so that the four-door family saloon of his goals becomes a two-door sports car! This is where preparation is so vital.

Bargaining

> **Frank** How does this sound? You can use the machine on Tuesdays and Thursdays, with overtime in the evenings. At other times I have priority and you should see me before logging on. We've agreed that my project has to be finished first, so if it is behind schedule at the end of the month, I'd like Tuesday afternoons as well.

During the bargaining phase, the aim is to arrive at a 'package', embracing all the issues which fall within the bargaining arena. This is where, provided the earlier stages have set the scene, the 'bluff' comes to the fore.

Bluff, threat and offer

For some people bluffing is seen as dishonesty; the reader must judge for himself. Bluffing involves committing yourself to a position in such a way that the other party believes you will only move from it reluctantly or not at all. The aim, at first, is to obtain greater concessions and make smaller ones. At some stage you must create the impression that your break point has been reached. If this is not true, have you been dishonest? In any event it is difficult to negotiate effectively without bluffing:

> **Jim** I think we should both have equal time allocated during normal hours.
> **Frank** No, Jim. I just cannot meet my project deadline if that happens.
> **Jim** You could do more overtime.
> **Frank** They won't approve payment if I do too much. I'm sure Malcolm (department manager) will support me on this.
> **Jim** OK, well how about if you have full use of the machine for three days?
> **Frank** I've worked out the figures, I need four.

Note the difference between Jim and Frank. Jim is not justifying his statements, he does not *commit* himself to a position. Frank, on the other hand, always gives a reason why he cannot move.

If you do not commit to a position, you can be easily pulled away from it. Another danger, however, is that you may commit too well. This may happen due to inexperience, a misreading of the situation (particularly an erroneous belief that you are in the bargaining arena), or a heightening of emotional tension leading to stubbornness. Deadlock involves a refusal of both parties to move from their respective positions or an inability to do so.

To avoid this position, it is usual to start with fairly low commitments and increase them as the break point approaches. Paradoxically, this means that the danger of deadlock increases the nearer a deal becomes! Sometimes it is possible to convince your opponent you are near your break point with a firm commitment early in the negotiations – but the hazards are obvious.

Bluff, then, does *not* mean formulating some unshakeable reason for sticking to a position. It is necessary to leave a way out – right up to the break point, or until you are convinced the bluff will work.

Specific bluff tactics must be tailored to the situation; some examples will show the principles:

Third party commitment – 'I've already told my wife I won't spend more than £1500 on a car, so that we can have a holiday.'

Policy commitment – 'It is against our policy to give discounts.'

Precedent commitment – 'If we concede on this point, all the other unions will demand similar improvements.'

Alternative – 'We could take our business elsewhere you know.'

None of these statements cannot be retreated from.

If, after making such commitments, the other party gains any ground at all, then they will feel they have won a considerable victory – the glue will have worked.

It is also possible to pull the other party towards you by the use of threats or other, more subtle, indications that direct power tactics are a feasible alternative to negotiation. A threat is best considered as a form of conditional bluff. It is successful, in negotiating terms, when it does not have to be carried out. Hence, as with the normal bluff, it is advisable to leave a loophole. In general, overt threats which are unsuccessful lead to a loss of credibility, so their use requires particular skill. Fisher states, perceptively, 'In most cases it is a mistake to attempt to influence the other side by making a negative commitment of any kind . . . it is a mistake to do so until one has first made the most of every other element of negotiating power.' (p. 16a).

Finally, in this analysis of the bargaining processes we should reiterate the common strategy of 'offer', noted earlier. This is use of 'if . . . then'. If you will do something, then I will do something; if you will concede that, then I will concede this. Offer is the core of the bargaining process; it is however more likely to be effective if supported by bluff or threat:

'I can only offer this because . . .'
'I will do this if you concede, but if you don't . . .'

There is another consideration to be made about the offers you make: always try to trade what is cheap for you to give, but valuable to the other party. This should be planned out at the preparation stage. For example, if you have specialist skills which make it easy to do favours for other managers, always think through how important the service which you provide is to them when asking for a return. It is a common failing to give away the most powerful bargaining tool simply by forgetting its true worth to the other side.

Close

Frank OK, we've agreed everything else; if you will just accept that the terminal should be moved into the vacant office, we've got a deal.

Frank Well, Jim, is it to be Tuesday mornings and Thursdays, or Mondays and Wednesday afternoons?

Frank Either you accept this suggestion, or we take the problem to higher authority. Which is it to be?

These are all potential 'closes'. When you have squeezed your opponent sufficiently, preferably not too much, then you must find a way to finish the process. The first example was a 'concession' close, the second an 'either/or' close, and the third an 'ultimatum' close. The latter, of course, is hazardous.

There are other alternatives, perhaps the commonest is the 'summary' close in which you just state what has been agreed. This process – agreeing – is an essential part of the closing stage. It is too easy to have a different impression of the deal from the other party. Sometimes you need to 'agree' in writing.

This final stage of negotiation carries particular emotional temptations. In the euphoria of the approaching conclusion it is too easy to make unnecessary concessions or to read into an agreement something which is not really there. Do not relax until you have parted company.

We opened this discussion on negotiation by identifying where it is most appropriate. Let us develop this a little further. Sometimes it is sound strategy to try to negotiate with an opponent who could otherwise use power directly to impose his will. Perhaps he would rather make some concessions than take the trouble to fight or risk the aftermath. Similar considerations apply if you are the party with most power – are you *sure* you can win without concessions?

Some issues, we must note, cannot be negotiated, such as deeply held beliefs or values, and issues to which we have already 'deadlocked' ourselves by prior commitment. If the other party is in this position, then we may overpower him or try to change his views, but he will not usually change them just because we make some concession in return.

Finally, let us summarize what Rubin calls the 'negotiation tightropes' which emphasize the dilemmas of the negotiator's art.[2] First, he must not be *too competitive*, or he risks deadlock. He must not be too *open and honest*, or he risks exploitation, but he must not be *too close or dishonest*, distrust may make negotiation impossible. He must balance *short-term gains* which may sour the relationship with *long-term gains*. Finally, he must *be sensitive*, so that he can read bluffs and identify goals, but *not oversensitive*, too weak or sympathetic.

The decision-making situation

Decision-making is one of the fundamental management activities, it has been researched and written about extensively from many viewpoints. A preliminary discussion of decision-making as a group process was presented in Chapter 4; our contribution in this section will be to develop the political dimension of decision-making.

Drucker[3] represents the solid core of management writers who prescribe a number of stages to be followed in making rational decisions. He suggests:

1 Defining the problem
2 Analysing the problem
3 Developing alternative solutions
4 Deciding upon the best solution
5 Converting the decision into effective action

No doubt sensible advice. If an individual is buying a house, for example, he should first define the problem:

● Why do I want a new house?
● What is wrong with my present accommodation?

He should go on to set objectives and identify constraints – price of house, number of bedrooms, and so on.

Analysing the problem involves activities such as gathering information, and identifying time constraints. In our example we might find out about mortgage costs, house prices, desirable locations and availability of schools.

Developing alternatives involves two stages – identification and evaluation. This is one of the areas in which most people spend too little time. They fail to explore a wide enough range of alternatives and often do not compare each, systematically, with their goals.

Having decided the best alternative, we now have to go ahead and implement the decision. This may need to be followed up by some kind of monitoring or evaluation process to see if we have really done the right thing.

There are several points at which this rational procedure tends to break down in practice. People often go straight for solutions without fully thinking through the early stages. Even where they attempt to try to think them through there are difficulties; symptoms can be mistaken for problems, information is ambiguous, or unavailable, or time-consuming or expensive to gather.

Audley[4] notes a further issue 'in choosing between two actions, A and B, man does not usually do as his modern logical or statistical counterpart would do, namely, ask whether A or B is the best action. Rather it is as if the processes governing our decisions first produced a statement like "I think A is right" and then looked for evidence in the light of this prior hypothesis . . . or to put it another way, minds quite often come already made up.'

Simon[5] argues that people do not try to optimize when making decisions, rather they search for alternatives until they find one which will meet their basic goals.

This process he calls 'satisficing', a word created from 'satisfy' and 'suffice'.

Much decision-making literature is concerned with quantitative and statistical techniques for gathering and analysing data. These techniques are often hard to apply in practice because they are slow, or because measurement is a problem, or because goals are not clearly defined. The techniques based on operations research, production management, statistics and other mathematical theories cannot make decisions; this is a human facility. Writers on these subjects try to overcome this limitation by *assuming* sets of goals for their techniques to optimize. Ansoff is an example: 'However measured and however variable, a set of objectives can be ascribed to each firm, and this set is the major guidepost in the decision process.'[6]

This kind of fudging is not necessary within the political framework where these techniques can be seen as aids to individuals or groups which can help them choose between strategies for pursuing *sectional* goals. If the techniques themselves, or goals specified within them, can be imposed on others, this may be a powerful influence mechanism in its own right.

An important omission from the rational decision-making stages so far discussed is any reference to other parties being involved. Even if we assume the perspective of the major decision maker we cannot necessarily carry out every stage entirely alone. We may need others to gather information, analyse data or give us the benefit of their knowledge and advice. We may need others to implement the decision willingly for it to succeed. Thus even if we have power to make decisions it may be sound strategy to involve others.

There are many levels of involvement, or participation, which a decision maker may allow. These range from keeping people informed at the lower end, to complete delegation. Figure 34 represents the considerations a decision maker may make.

He will need to assess whether the parties to be involved will have similar values and objectives to each other and to himself. Will consensus be easy to reach, or will some weak compromise be the most likely outcome? Can the involvement process provide an opportunity to win people over?

Time is always a factor in decision-making. Achieving consensus may be a lengthy process. It may be quicker, however, than a unilateral decision which leads to conflict and cannot be implemented. Sometimes involving people can also save time, because they have important knowledge within the group which they would otherwise have to search for.

Involving people can be costly. There is always a trade-off between decision quality, time and the need for acceptance. Sometimes it is better to make a decision alone, even if it is marginally wrong, than spend hours discussing it. It is not important if we spend an extra ten pence a week on pencils because we do not locate the cheapest supplier.

If the decision must be high quality, then we need to know whether we are capable of making it alone and how much time is available. Will others be capable and committed if they are asked to help?

Thus the six considerations in Figure 34 must be balanced by the decision

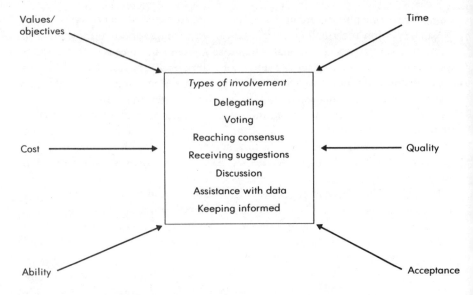

Figure 34   *Involvement in decisions*

maker when he chooses how much to involve others. But this assumes he is in the powerful role. Much of a manager's time is not spent decision-making, but rather is spent on other people's decisions or as part of organizational decision-making systems. The following analysis provides a framework for gaining political insight into this type of activity.

Affecting the decision process

Accepting that many decisions will not involve all of them, we shall consider nine elements in a full decision process:

1 Define the problem
2 Decide the process
3 Decide the parties involved
4 Analyse the problem and gather information
5 Formulate goals
6 Develop alternatives
7 Decide the best solution
8 Implement
9 Evaluate outcomes

Decision-making is not a linear progression through these stages; they may be carried out in different sequences, often at the same time, or in loops. For example, we may set goals fairly early in the process but when evaluating alternatives we may find them unattainable. Also, we may unearth data which forces us to redefine the problem. We may have unforeseen difficulties at the implementation stage, which show that a previously rejected alternative is preferable.

A manager, concerned with the politics of organizations, must be aware of the possibilities for affecting each stage of the process.

Define the problem

Tommyrot Ltd are in trouble. Their sales are down, delivery dates are not being met, the workforce is unsettled, financial breakdown is looming. The senior executives are involved in serious discussion:

Marketing Director   We have got to cut our prices and we can't do that until we get costs down. Furthermore (to the production director), you have got to improve efficiency and get orders out on time.

Production Director   Throughput time is high because of all the industrial relations problems. We must sort out the bonus scheme and do something about job grading. The present systems are obviously unfair. Sorting these things out would get costs down too, but we also need new machinery in the main fabrication shop.

Financial Director   Any change in the bonus scheme would cost money, so would new machinery. It is just not available; our real problem is lack of cash.

These managers are trying to influence the definition of Tommyrot's problems in order to make their own lives easier and also, perhaps, to avoid personal blame. The *symptoms* are clear – sales down, poor delivery, industrial strife, financial difficulties – but what is the underlying problem? If the production director, for example, can convince the others that the bonus and job grading systems are the real areas to sort out, then his life may be made much easier and the personnel department may shoulder the responsibility.

Decide the process and the parties involved

Managing Director   I have no idea which of you is right, so I'm going to call in Brainbox, the consultants, and ask them to do a study. I'd like you all to prepare reports identifying your own problems and suggesting solutions.

The marketing director smiled. He had worked with Brainbox before and was sure he could influence their report.

The managing director of Tommyrot is in a difficult position. All the parties involved in the decision have sectional axes to grind. He clearly hopes that a firm of consultants will provide an impartial analysis of the problem.

The nature of the decision process is crucial:

What should the time scale be?
Should the decision be made by one manager?
Should it be a committee?
Should a working party prepare a report?

Financial Director   Brainbox are very expensive. I suggest that we set up a small 'in house' group to look at the problems. My deputy would be the ideal person to head such a group.

This may sound like a rational statement, but it is in fact a political manoeuvre designed to influence the ultimate decision in favour of the finance function. The financial director may have particular confidence in the ability of his deputy to influence others in a small group, and by putting him in the role of leader, and probably report writer, he increases his influence still further.

Analyse the problem/gather information/develop alternatives
In these related phases of the decision process we can easily imagine the political processes which take place. People provide information in a form which they hope will favour their preferred outcomes. Those involved in the decision look for data which confirms their views; they accept or reject suggestions and information on the basis of their own perceptions, values and goals.

In most decisions the range of alternatives considered is far smaller than it might be. It is possible to influence ultimate outcomes by restricting the alternatives to those which are favourable, or perhaps by considering one favourable possibility and a range of others which will be rejected by all parties. Obvious examples here are the process of shortlisting for jobs and the selection of items for discussion at a meeting, but the same idea applies to all decisions.

Formulate goals/evaluate alternatives/decide the best solution
Personnel Director   This working party report implies that the only things we have to worry about are costs, delivery dates and profits. I knew it was a mistake not to have a personnel specialist in the group. You have to consider the workforce, they have rights and they are the people who, in the end, will have to work with any changes.

If you can influence the goals being pursued in the decision process, then you will inevitably influence the way alternatives are evaluated and the selection of the 'best' alternative. Managers are usually conditioned to accept managerialist goals, although they may interpret them in different ways to suit their sectional interests. For example, the marketing director may suggest increasing advertising expenditure to increase profits, whereas the production director may want new equipment. Each believes, or at least claims, that what is best for him is also best for the organization.

Implement
It is at the implementation stage that a failure to involve powerful groups in the decision process may be regretted. The personnel director at Tommyrot is clearly concerned about the idea of just introducing major changes without consulting the workforce.

Even those who have been consulted but whose preferred outcome was not achieved may cause difficulties if they fail to co-operate in the implementation.

Evaluate

Any kind of monitoring or evaluation of organizational decisions is comparatively rare. For many decisions the effort and expense would simply not be justified. For others it is too late. Evaluation might show where the mistake was made but this may not be useful; perhaps it is better to direct energies to correcting the new situation.

An important reason for non-evaluation is that it is often impossible. If we recruit X instead of Y, and X is not a great success, how can we know whether Y would have been any better?

There is also the question of blame. Evaluating decisions might show up inadequacies of those involved. If those people are in powerful positions they will probably find 'rational' reasons to resist any idea of an inquiry. In any event, as all government politicians know, even where an inquiry is held, it is quite possible for powerful figures to influence the outcome in their favour.

Interpersonal skills

Within almost any influence strategy there will come a time when an actor must interact with others on an interpersonal level. Sometimes an apparently sound strategy may fail because you fail to persuade someone about your ideas, or you annoy someone, or they respond to you in some other undesirable way. Thus there is a need to think about the interpersonal tactics which may operate within a particular strategy.

Social behaviour involves both verbal and non-verbal communication. Bodily contact, proximity, head movements, facial expressions, gestures, bodily posture, even direction of gaze and physical appearance are all important ways in which we indicate our feelings and elicit responses from others. Even in verbal communications we can vary the message, using the same words but different voice levels or emotional emphases. We should also note the important links which exist between methods of communication. A sentence said with a smile may mean the exact opposite if said with a shake of the fist.

The intricacies of behavioural skills cannot be tackled in detail in this book. Writers in the field, however, are becoming aware of the importance of their subject in political terms. Sidney *et al*[9] ask 'Do social skills entail manipulation?' Their answer is a clear 'yes' but they emphasize that this does not mean skills training is unethical; social skills are used by everyone, trained or not. The fact is that social skills, like any other skills, can be used for 'good' or 'evil' purposes.

We shall examine two helpful approaches to thinking about interactions, behavioural analysis and transactional analysis. Both approaches make the assumption that our behaviour significantly affects that of others with whom we

Figure 35   *Behaviour analysis*

Proposing behaviour	Suggesting actions. e.g. 'Let's go to the pictures.'
Development behaviour	Building on proposals made by others. Supporting the ideas of others. Bringing others into consideration. e.g 'Yes, green would be great for the wall, and we could use cream for the ceiling.'
Reasoned negative behaviour	Disagreeing with others in a reasoned way. Stating difficulties with their ideas. e.g. 'But price can't be the problem because their product costs even more.'
Emotional negative behaviour	Attacking others. Being critical. Defending against such attacks in the same emotional way. e.g. 'Rubbish.'
Clarifying behaviour	Checking whether people understand. Summarizing previous discussions. e.g. 'As I see it, this is what we've agreed.'
Seeking information behaviour	Seeking facts, opinions, ideas. e.g. 'How much discount for cash?'
Giving information behaviour	Giving facts, opinions, ideas. e.g. 'We have fifteen minutes left.'

interact in face-to-face situations. Conversely, of course, their behaviour affects us.

Behaviour analysis

If I shout at a colleague he will most likely shout back. If I ask him a question he will most likely give me an answer. If I support a statement he has just made and develop it a little further he will most likely not reject my idea out of hand.

From an examination of these simple statements we can make a fundamental point. If by changing my behaviour I can obtain different responses from people, then, provided I can control this process well enough, it can be a useful influence tactic. The first problem is to categorize behaviours.

Different authorities identify a range of behaviour types. Inevitably they will always be too few to cope with reality. For the purposes of explanation, we shall discuss the seven categories outlined in Figure 35.

Behaviour analysis copes best with verbal interactions and is specifically helpful in understanding processes in committees and other groups discussions where they predominate. Nevertheless, non-verbal behaviours such as facial expressions, arm and body movements and even dress can affect the interpretations of any action.

Having shown that behaviours can be categorized into types with particular characteristics, our problem is how to identify the likely responses which each category can evoke. This is something we have all been doing since we were very young. It is instinctive, and yet some people are very much more effective in interpersonal situations than others. An explicit awareness of the processes taking place may be the first step to personal development.

Peter Honey[7] has studied the relationships between different behaviours and their most common responses. His categories are slightly different from ours but we have been able to draw conclusions from his analysis:

Proposing behaviours usually elicit either development behaviour in the form of support, or reasoned negative behaviour in the form of some kind of difficulty stating.

Development behaviours usually lead to further development or perhaps a question asking for further explanation.

Reasoned negative behaviours tend to evoke similar negative behaviours in response. I disagree with you, you disagree with me; this can be a downward spiral in terms of communication and emotions. The way to avoid this spiral is to state difficulties and identify differences as reasonably as possible, perhaps even as questions. Verbal or non-verbal methods can be used to emphasize that you are really on the same side.

Emotional negative behaviours can be summarized basically as attacking and defending. In general, attack begets either attack or defence. It can be hard to return to constructive interaction.

Clarifying behaviour tends to lead to supportive, development behaviour, although there can also, of course, be disagreement.

Seeking information behaviour almost always evokes giving information. The certainty of response makes this a powerful shaping behaviour.

Giving information behaviour is usually a response to other behaviours, especially seeking information. It is uncertain in its effects, since this depends largely on the content of the statement.

What can the political actor learn from these simple generalizations? Clearly no specific advice on how to handle a unique situation emerges. But the main point is that we must arrange our outward behaviour so that it has the desired effect on those with whom we are interacting. The 'desired effect' will depend on our goals. If we want to persuade someone to our way of thinking, then development behaviours are more likely to be effective than emotional disagreement. If we want to influence a group, then we will find proposing and giving information behaviours cannot be avoided. Sometimes, however, it is better to introduce a subject by seeking rather than giving information about it. The response mode is more certain. If we have to disagree with others we should be aware of the different methods of doing so. Do we really want to attack?

Certain behaviour modes relate to different roles in the group. If we use clarifiying behaviour frequently we can informally adopt a type of chairperson position. If we are frequently negative we may isolate ourselves. Development behaviours draw us into the group. Seeking information shows that we do not consider ourselves all-knowing and that we respect the views of others. Too much giving information may have the reverse effect.

Behaviour analysis helps us not only to think about our own behaviour but also about the behaviour of others. If we sense that there is too much unproductive information giving going on within a group activity, then we can try to encourage more listening, either by discussing the problem, or by using clarifying behaviour to consolidate progress, or by asking questions. Thus we can be aware of the antidotes which can be used to change undesirable behaviour in others. If someone is attacking, we do not have to attack in response, we can support them or, perhaps more likely, we could reduce the emotional level by asking for a more detailed, reasonable explanation of their position.

Finally, let us note that the context, the power of the actors and their prior relationships, cannot be divorced from the behaviour process. The type of behaviour we can use and the type of response it will evoke is not merely dependent on the behaviour itself.

Transactional analysis

Transactional analysis is an approach to understanding social psychological behaviour which originated in the 1950s with Dr Eric Berne.[8] As will become evident, it is much more sophisticated and comprehensive than behaviour analysis and thus potentially more useful to the political actor in a wide range of interpersonal situations. Berne's approach, like behaviour analysis, seeks to help us understand social interactions, but it extends deeper into the psychological processes behind them.

The unit of social interaction is called a transaction: 'If two or more people encounter each other . . . sooner or later one of them will speak, or give some other indication of acknowledging the presence of the others. This is called the *transactional stimulus*. Another person will then say or do something which is in some way related to the stimulus, and that is called the *transactional response* . . . transactions tend to proceed in chains, so that each response is in turn a stimulus.' (p. 29)

Transactional analysis is a method for examining the relationships between transactions and for explaining and predicting patterns which occur.

The psychological theory behind transactional analysis rests on the idea that we respond to each other in terms of three main 'ego states'. An ego state is a pattern of feelings, a frame of mind which leads to a certain type of behaviour. We may distinguish Parent, Adult and Child ego states.

The 'Parent' state reflects all that we learned in our early childhood. The 'nos', the 'don'ts', the morals, the praise, the restriction, the help, the care – all these aspects of our parents' behaviour are recorded in our subconscious. The 'Child' state also reflects our early childhood, but instead of the *external* stimuli from our parents it is based on our *internal* feelings at the time. Basically, the Child state exists when we are acting on the basis of our emotions rather than our reason. This does not mean the Child is a negative condition. It sometimes involves guilt, frustration and anger, but also love, sensuality and excitement. In the Child reside the origins of creativity and curiosity.

The 'Adult' state results from our conscious abilities to think and to behave. Throughout our lives we gather and process data, we formulate ideas and compare them with our experiences. We make judgements, we reason, we decide. The Adult within us may moderate the effects on our behaviour of both the Parent and the Child as well as influencing our behaviour directly.

A short conversation will provide us with some examples:

(1) **Tom** Mike, I've told you to stop smoking. That cough is getting worse.
(2) **Mike** I don't believe it's the smoking that's making me cough, I've got a cold.
(3) **Tom** Do as you're told and put that cigarette out.
(4) **Mike** Go to hell!
(5) **Tom** You're an intransigent sod.
(6) **Mike** I'll tell you what, if you'll make us a cup of tea, I won't smoke any more today.

We hope that the reader can already categorize these transactions. (1) is clearly Parent. Mike could have responded by accepting the command or perhaps rejecting it aggressively (Child responses), but he chose an Adult mode. In (3) Tom continues his Parent behaviour and this time provokes an emotional Child riposte. Instead of trying the Parent for a third time, Tom, perhaps frustrated by his lack of success at influencing Mike, expresses this emotion in (5). The response from Mike is to switch back to the Adult state and offer a compromise.

The reader should try a few examples of his own. Anticipate going home one evening and demanding a meal 'at once', what response would this evoke? Would it most likely be in the Parent, Adult or Child mode? How would your next statement affect the course of events?

Everyone is, to some extent, capable of switching from one ego state to another. For some the switching can be better controlled than others, depending on the strength of the different states in the individual's psychological make-up. If we are trying to affect the behaviour of others, it is most useful to develop the skill of strategic switching of behaviour modes.

Consider another example: Jane has just had her request for a wage increase turned down; she does not want to give up, so determines to continue the conversation. How would a Parent transaction sound?

'You're making a mistake you know. It's important to keep up staff morale and this is one step in the right direction.'

Or an Adult transaction?

'I have earned a rise. My success with that project has had a big impact on the department's image.'

Or Child?

'I *want* a rise, it's not fair.'

The likely response depends, of course, on prior relationships and the whole range of political forces. Nevertheless, we can see that those forces do not *determine* the response. The approach from Jane *has* to be right.

Different behaviours lead to different feelings and different responses. Assume you have adopted the Parent stance and instructed a friend to do something for you:

'Pour me a drink.'
'OK.'

'Pour me a drink.'
'Why?'

'Pour me a drink.'
'Do it yourself.'

'Pour me a drink.'
'You know it isn't good for you.'

How do you feel after each reply? Which ego state will you now adopt in order to get the drink?

When we are involved in a social situation it is too easy just to respond to our Parent, Adult and Child states as they emerge during the interaction. If we are pursuing objectives in the social situation then we need to actively choose appropriate behaviour patterns.

There is clearly much more to transactional analysis than we have been able to convey in this brief outline. The reader is encouraged to find out more by referring to the previously quoted work of Berne and/or the later work of Harris.[10]

There is also much more to learn about interpersonal skills than the two approaches we have introduced; our primary purpose has not been to teach social skills but to emphasize their importance to the political actor. A recent text edited by Cooper[11] contains descriptions of four techniques – transactional analysis, interaction analysis, assertiveness training and T-groups – and an excellent comparative evaluation. It must be said, however, that all these approaches offer only partial insights into the true complexity of human relationships.

In this chapter we have focused on negotiation, decision-making and face-to-face interaction, all specific political situations on which there are growing literatures. Instinct and experience tell us that there is much more still to be learned about these situations and also that there are many others which would fruitfully repay study. Everything from promotion processes to budgetary control and from product development to plant layout can be characterized as a political situation. The approach described in this book would be a useful research framework. Our primary hope, however, is that it will prove helpful to the future manager.

References
1   R. Fisher, 'Negotiating power-getting and using influence', *American Behavioral Scientist*, vol. 27, no. 2 (November/December 1983), pp. 149–67
2   J. Rubin, 'Negotiation: an introduction to some issues and themes', *American Behavioral Scientist*, vol. 27, no. 2 (November/December 1983), pp. 135–47
3   P. Drucker, *The Practice of Management* (New York: Harper and Row 1954)
4   R. Audley, 'What makes up a mind?', from F. Castles *et al*, *Decisions, Organizations and Society* (Penguin 1971)
5   H. Simon, 'Theories in decision-making in economics and behavioral sciences', *American Economic Review*, vol. 49, no. 3 (June 1959). pp. 253–83
6   H.I. Ansoff, *Corporate Strategy* (Penguin 1968)
7   P. Honey, *Face to Face, A Practical Guide to Interactive Skills* (Institute of Personnel Management 1976)
8   E. Berne, *Games People Play* (Penguin 1968)
9   E. Sidney *et al*, *Skills with People* (Business Books 1973)
10   T. Harris, *I'm OK – You're OK* (Pan 1973)
11   C. Cooper (ed.), *Improving Interpersonal Relations* (Gower 1981)

EPILOGUE _____

In Part One we developed the foundations for understanding OB by learning about the underlying organization theories from which the major concepts have emerged and in which many modern ideas are still embedded. In Part Two we explored some central concerns of OB: individual motivation, group behaviour and organization structures, cultures and climates. We showed how the political perspective offers new insights into these important subjects. In Part Three we built a theory of political behaviour in organizations. We showed how the bases of power, the context of the political process and the strategies adopted by different actors are related. We delved into each component of our model, developing language and ideas as we went, using simple examples at every opportunity. We hope that by now the reader is well equipped to contemplate his place in the political milieu and to actively influence the behaviour of others.

However, there is one vital matter which has not yet been broached, indeed we have deliberately set it aside in order to develop the political model without inhibition. This is the matter of ethics, of values, of morality, of responsibility, of equity, of justice – we shall not pursue the semantics. But it would be remiss in a text of this nature to sidestep altogether the issue of how people *should* behave.

In the literature, questions of ethics are often dealt with at the corporate level: 'How should *companies* behave?' In keeping with the perspective of this book, however, we would rather ask 'How should *people* behave, what values and principles should guide them?'

An individual, as we have noted at various points in the text, almost always eliminates some alternatives for ethical reasons. He does not commit murder, he may not lie, he may choose not to give preferential treatment to friends or to discriminate on the grounds of race. Ethics apply constraints to our strategy-making. They may also give strategy its direction; our beliefs affect the goals we choose to follow.

Management is not just a rat race in which the law of the jungle predominates. Many managers are prepared to make personal sacrifices in support of their views. A true measure of a manager's integrity is not simply the consistency with which he applies his morality but also the degree of suffering he is prepared to face by doing so.

The conventional textbook approach is to tell the manager that he has responsibilities to owners, workers, customers, suppliers and society (and often other groups too), and leave him with the problem of balancing their conflicting interests. This is a considerable burden. It cannot be solved in practice by exhorting the manager to do 'the greatest good for the greatest number'. Neither 'good' nor 'number' are viable concepts.

The individual clearly has to make decisions. Some alternatives he can eliminate as violating his deeply held beliefs. Others will have to be weighed against each other. This is the agonizing process of coping with moral dilemmas that all managers have to face. Should I recommend for redundancy those who are least efficient or those who will suffer least? Should I work for a company that sells cigarettes? Should I lie as part of negotiating strategy? Most choices have good *and* bad outcomes, they are ethically justifiable from some points of view but not from others. And, of course, the manager has his personal interests to consider.

Managers may make less ethical decisions for a number of reasons. First, decisions in organizations are often made in stages, or by committees, or by teams, based on reports, recommendations, etc. No one manager feels personally responsible. Then there is the tendency to play the role game, 'I don't make this decision as an individual but as a production manager', thus sidestepping the pain of an unethical choice. Another problem is that of the corporate culture which often values company loyalty above ethical behaviour of any other kind, so that the individual may justify almost anything, whoever it hurts, because it is good for the company. Organizations often operate in such a way that promotion will only be earned by those who do not question difficult ethical issues.

There are two further problems which may reduce managerial ethics to lower levels than may be desirable. Managers often do not have to carry out their decisions and, on occasion, may even be unaware of their consequences. A manager who calls for reductions in material quality to cut costs may not be aware when five years later there is an unpleasant accident.

But perhaps the most important reason for ethical failings in organizations is that such considerations are largely ignored in management training. This is not the appropriate place to start what would need to be a second volume. Let us merely note that very few managers have, at any stage in their development, been made aware of the range of ethical stances they might adopt or the dilemmas they will face, nor have they been encouraged to work out their own moral beliefs so that they can act with integrity, at least in the sense of being true to themselves. On the contrary, most management training simply assumes that decisions can be made after a systematic analysis of the alternatives in terms of managerialist criteria.

The starting point for moral awareness is for the manager to ask himself this question:

'Should I simply carry out instructions and comply with rules, procedures and systems?

If the answer is 'yes' then life will be very simple. If there is any doubt in the manager's mind, then let him ask:

'Should I take a positive stance, think through my own beliefs and evaluate any instructions, rules, procedures and systems in the light of them?'

If the answer to this question is 'yes' then the reader has embarked on a lifelong quest for integrity which, in our view, is the very essence of a pluralist, democratic society. We hope you will find the political insights gained in this text of use in your battles with those of lesser honour.

INDEX